Presented to

_____

on the occasion of

_____

from

_____

Entertaining
with Friends
cookbook

MONROE CARELL JR. CHILDREN'S HOSPITAL AT VANDERBILT

Entertaining
with Friends

cookbook

MONROE CARELL JR. CHILDREN'S HOSPITAL AT VANDERBILT

Entertaining with Friends

Published by Monroe Carell Jr. Children's Hospital at Vanderbilt
Copyright 2006
Monroe Carell Jr. Children's Hospital at Vanderbilt
2200 Children's Way
Nashville, Tennessee 37232

Photography: Jacket, cover, food photography and page 10 © Mark Boughton Photography, Nashville, Tennessee;
pages 5, 7, 9, 11 and 13 © Mark Tucker, Nashville, Tennessee;
flap photography, Dana Johnson © Vanderbilt University.

Project Management: Development Office of Monroe Carell Jr. Children's Hospital at Vanderbilt

Additional copies of *Entertaining with Friends* may be obtained by contacting:
Friends of Monroe Carell Jr. Children's Hospital at Vanderbilt
2525 West End, Suite 450
Nashville, Tennessee 37203
615-322-7450
e-mail address: www.vanderbiltchildrens.com

This cookbook is a collection of favorite recipes, which are not necessarily original recipes.

Friends of Children's Hospital made every effort to verify the time line for accuracy.
We apologize for any errors or omissions.

Library of Congress Number: 2005927470
ISBN: 0-9766884-0-9

Edited, Designed, and Manufactured by
Favorite Recipes® Press
An imprint of

FRP

PO Box 305142, Nashville, Tennessee 37230
1-800-358-0560

Cookbook Committee

Chairman: Peggy Franks
Recipe Testing: Abby McLemore
Recipe Development/Coordination: Terrie Purser

Art/Design: Susan Basel
Research/Non-recipe Text: Claudia McLemore
Entertainment: Anne Saint

Art Director: Steve Newman
Managing Editor: Mary Cummings
Project Coordinator: Ashley Bienvenu

Book Designer: David Malone
Project Editor: Susan Larson
Operations Director: Ed Arndt

Manufactured in China
First Printing 2006   20,000 copies

Dedication

This book is dedicated to the patients of the Monroe Carell Jr. Children's Hospital at Vanderbilt who inspire us with their beauty and courage, and to the staff and volunteers who serve them with talent and passion.

a collection
of recipes
to celebrate
with friends

Table of Contents

8 – Hospital History

9 – The Children's Fund

10 – Word of Thanks

11 – Preface

12 – Friends History

14 – Great Beginnings

40 – Salads & Soups

64 – Let's Do Brunch

90 – Dinner Is Served

132 – The Great Outdoors

152 – Children's Favorites

174 – Eat Your Vegetables

190 – Sweet Endings

232 – Acknowledgments

233 – Contributors

235 – Index

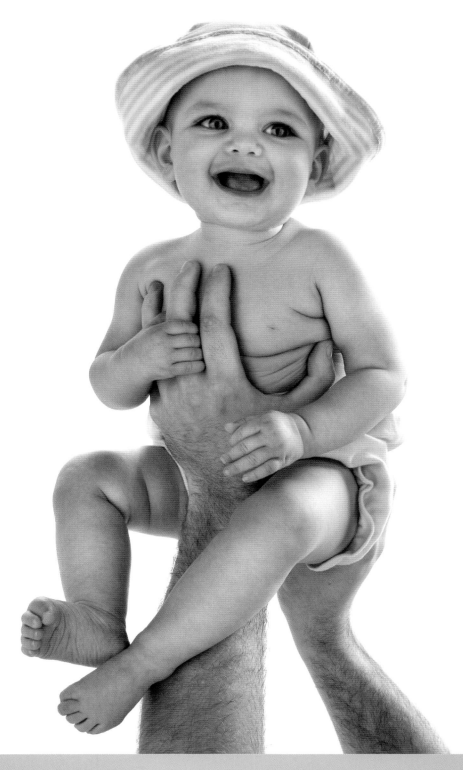

Hospital History

Long before the state-of-the-art Monroe Carell Jr. Children's Hospital at Vanderbilt opened its doors in February 2004, Vanderbilt medical professionals understood the importance of specialized pediatric care. They knew that the physical and emotional needs of sick and injured children were very different from those of adults. So they worked diligently to treat their young patients with special care. With this approach in mind, Vanderbilt Hospital began operating collaboratively with the Junior League Home, which was sponsored by the Junior League of Nashville to provide convalescent and rehabilitative care for children with crippling orthopedic diseases, regardless of ability to pay.

By the late 1960s, healthcare experts recognized that children needed not only special treatment, but also a special environment. Dr. David T. Karzon, chairman and medical director of the Department of Pediatrics, led an effort to create a "hospital within a hospital" for young patients at Vanderbilt. The concept was adopted in 1970 and became the Children's Regional Medical Center, specially designed to meet the medical needs of children while providing access to the sophisticated technology of the main hospital. The Junior League Home moved to the Children's Center, where it broadened its services while maintaining its commitment to underwrite pediatric medical care. The Children's Center was renamed Vanderbilt Children's Hospital.

Dr. Ian Burr, who succeeded Dr. Karzon as medical director in 1988, guided the Children's Hospital as it grew to offer treatment in more than twenty-nine subspecialties. It soon became clear that a freestanding hospital devoted entirely to children's care was needed. After five years of careful planning to fully understand the needs of physicians and children and their families, construction began on the Monroe Carell Jr. Children's Hospital at Vanderbilt.

Throughout the decades, Vanderbilt Children's Hospital has remained loyal to its original mission. Its medical pioneers have developed new vaccines, treatments, and techniques. The facility is recognized worldwide as a top center for the treatment of childhood cancers. Its advocacy programs for car safety seats, injury prevention, childhood immunization, and other initiatives have impacted the lives of countless children across the region. Most importantly, the Children's Hospital has provided children and their families with hope for a better tomorrow.

The Children's Fund

All money raised through the sale of *Entertaining with Friends* will directly benefit The Children's Fund, which supports the care of all young patients served by the Monroe Carell Jr. Children's Hospital at Vanderbilt.

Established in 1970 with the opening of the Children's Hospital, The Children's Fund is a special interest-bearing account that receives donations from individuals, schools, special events, businesses, foundations, and organizations throughout Middle Tennessee, Southern Kentucky, and Northern Alabama.

In recent years The Children's Fund has helped underwrite construction of the new Doctors' Office Tower, finance cutting-edge clinical research, and develop specialized programs, such as the Eating Disorders Clinic and safety and prevention initiatives. Most importantly, gifts to the fund allow the hospital to provide the highest quality medical care to any child, regardless of a family's ability to pay.

A Word of Thanks

All of us at Monroe Carell Jr. Children's Hospital at Vanderbilt extend our gratitude to the many contributors to this cookbook. These recipes represent a true slice of our community. Some are served by Nashville's most recognized chefs, while others are prepared in the kitchens of our friends and neighbors, which is fitting. For throughout its history Vanderbilt Children's Hospital has been a vital resource for young patients and their families from all walks of life. We especially appreciate those who shared stories of their experiences at the hospital. Such kind words not only enable us to see the true impact of our work on the lives of others, they serve as an immeasurable source of encouragement as we continue our mission.

Finally, very special thanks to the Friends of Monroe Carell Jr. Children's Hospital at Vanderbilt, particularly to the cookbook committee—Peggy Franks, Susan Basel, Terrie Purser, Claudia McLemore, Abby McLemore, and Anne Saint—for their time and dedication. They not only developed the concept for the cookbook and served as tireless champions to see it through, but they also prepared and tested over one thousand recipes.

This cookbook is truly a labor of love, and we are fortunate to have so many friends who care so deeply about our work and the people we serve.

Preface

Certainly, the new Monroe Carell Jr. Children's Hospital at Vanderbilt is a testament to innovation and leadership in health care. But at its core, the hospital is about family. Its design specifically recognizes that families are vital members of a health care team, essential to a child's healing process.

That's why we emphasize the concepts of family and fellowship in this cookbook. While some of the recipes have been lovingly contributed by friends, others are from families whose lives have been touched in some way by the hospital. Several came with notes, telling us how a special dish brightened the mood of a sick child or how familiar food comforted a young patient in unfamiliar surroundings. Some wrote of how a festive meal was the center of a celebration of recovery, while others shared a favorite recipe in memory of a loved one now gone.

In these pages, you will find recipes ranging from a simple snack a child can make with a friend, to an elaborate entrée for a large and elegant gathering. But they all reflect our need for family and the promise that a good meal can bring us together with the people we love.

The Cookbook Committee
Peggy Franks
Susan Basel
Abby McLemore
Claudia McLemore
Terrie Purser
Anne Saint

Friends History

In 1973, soon after the Children's Hospital was established, local volunteer community leaders asked for a meeting with Dr. David T. Karzon, the hospital's medical director. They proposed creating a volunteer group to support the hospital through fund-raising and public awareness activities. With the blessing of the Vanderbilt Board of Trust, Friends of the Children's Hospital at Vanderbilt was formed.

Libby Werthan served as the first president of the Friends and its sixty-seven founding members. By the end of its first year, membership grew to 265. Today there are more than two thousand members and five chapters of Friends working tirelessly to realize the goals of the organization.

Their efforts are far-reaching. Although the Monroe Carell Jr. Children's Hospital at Vanderbilt is located in Davidson County, it is truly a regional facility, serving children and families in Middle Tennessee, Southern Kentucky, and Northern Alabama. Local chapters of the Friends in Williamson, Rutherford, Maury, and Montgomery counties have been established to focus fund-raising and ensure that people in these communities are aware of the unique and vital services the Children's Hospital has to offer.

The Friends continued its tradition of raising funds for the hospital through the Palm Sunday Paper Sale. In the spring of 1973, *The Tennessean* began printing a special annual supplemental section focusing on the work of Vanderbilt Children's Hospital, sold door-to-door by Friends and other volunteers. All told, the Palm Sunday Paper Sale has raised more than $2 million.

The Holiday Project, also begun in 1973 and now one of the area's most anticipated events of the season, has been another fund-raising success for the Friends. Over the years, the sale of holiday cards and gift tags, featuring designs created by young patients at the Children's Hospital, has raised more than $600,000.

One of Nashville's true signature events, The Iroquois Steeplechase has benefited the Children's Hospital since 1981. Held at the equestrian area of Warner Parks since 1941, this rite of spring draws thousands of horse racing enthusiasts and hospital supporters each year.

Volunteers from the Friends of Vanderbilt Children's Hospital produce the race and its ancillary social functions, helping to improve the course, facilities, and purses. Most importantly, in the past quarter century, the Steeplechase has grown to become the single-largest event contributor to Vanderbilt Children's Hospital.

The Friends also provide the volunteer support for Children's Miracle Network. Vanderbilt Children's Hospital was one of the founding members of the network, which includes twenty-two children's hospitals across the country. The network's annual national telethon attracts millions of viewers in the Middle Tennessee region, serving as an educational and fund-raising vehicle. In 1983, its first year, the telethon raised more than $80,000 for Children's Hospital. Total telethon contributions to Vanderbilt Children's Hospital have grown to more than $12 million, due in large part to the support of News Channel 5-WTVF and other local sponsors.

In addition to fund-raising, the Friends are also extensively involved in the life of the hospital, continually re-examining needs to find ways to enhance services for children and their families. Members organize Valentine's, Easter, and holiday parties for the children, plus a "Sports Day" in October and "Beach Day" in February. Once a month, they deliver hot dinners and breakfasts to families of hospitalized children. They provide reading materials and nonperishable snacks in the family lounges and host parties for the staff.

Friends also provide educational materials to use in classrooms and assist at Health and Safety Fairs. And many members also volunteer in the hospital activity rooms and patient units.

These are just some examples of the work of the Friends of Monroe Carell Jr. Children's Hospital at Vanderbilt. And its first thirty years are only the beginning. As the hospital continues to carry out its mission, the Friends are more committed than ever to finding new and creative ways to support this irreplaceable community resource.

Great Beginnings

chapter one

Asparagus Roll-ups

Avocado Salsa

Warm Blue Cheese and Bacon Dip

Blue Cheese Puffs

Nutty Napoleons

Cream Cheese and Feta Spread

Mexican Cheesecake

Chèvre Champignons

Goat Cheese Crisps

Tomato and Goat Cheese Crostini

Roasted Eggplant Spread

Green and Red Pepper Jelly Spread

Vidalia Onion Spread

Tomato and Onion Tart

Spinach Dip with Pita Chips

Spicy Egg Rolls with Creamy Cilantro
Dipping Sauce

Reuben Dip

Chicken Salad in Cucumber Cups

Creamy Deviled Eggs

Smoked Salmon and Egg Salad

Smoked Trout Mousse on Endive

Salmon and Hearts of Palm Rolls

Cold Crab Salad

Creamy Hot Crab Dip

Eastern Shore Crab Cakes

Chef Ray's Tropical Rock Shrimp Salsa

Marinated Shrimp

Savory Tortilla Chips

Ben's Favorite Dip

Asparagus Roll-Ups

Bored with crudités? Try jicama, a Latin root vegetable that can be eaten raw or cooked. It has the texture of a raw potato and is usually very sweet. Serve sliced, with lime juice drizzled atop and sprinkled with chili pepper. It is also delicious added to salsas or grilled with olive oil next time you cook out.

1 loaf white or wheat bread, cut into 30 slices and crusts trimmed
8 ounces light cream cheese, softened
1/4 cup mayonnaise
1 tablespoon minced fresh chives
1/2 teaspoon Morton Nature's Seasons Seasoning Blend
2 (15-ounce) cans asparagus spears, drained
1/4 cup (1/2 stick) butter, melted
1/4 cup grated Parmesan cheese
Paprika

Preheat the oven to 400 degrees. Flatten each bread slice with a rolling pin. Mix the cream cheese, mayonnaise, chives and seasoning blend in a bowl. Spread the cream cheese mixture over the bread slices, covering completely. Place 1 asparagus spear on each bread slice and roll as for a jelly roll. Place the roll-ups seam side down on a greased baking sheet. Brush with the butter and sprinkle with the Parmesan cheese and paprika. Bake for 12 minutes.

Yield: 30 roll-ups

Avocado Salsa

2 ripe avocados, chopped
2 ripe tomatoes, chopped
3 or 4 green onions, chopped
2 mushrooms, sliced
1 (4-ounce) can chopped green chiles
1 (3-ounce) can chopped black olives, drained
2 tablespoons canola oil
1 tablespoon olive oil
1 1/2 tablespoons red wine vinegar
1 teaspoon garlic salt
1/2 teaspoon pepper
Tortilla chips

Combine the avocados, tomatoes, green onions, mushrooms, green chiles, olives, canola oil, olive oil, vinegar, garlic salt and pepper in a bowl and mix well. Serve with tortilla chips.

Note: Prepare the salsa a day ahead—the flavor only gets better.

Yield: 6 servings

Warm Blue Cheese and Bacon Dip

7 slices bacon, chopped
2 garlic cloves, minced
8 ounces cream cheese, softened
1/4 cup half-and-half
4 ounces blue cheese, crumbled
2 tablespoons chopped fresh chives
3 tablespoons (about 1 ounce)
    chopped smoked almonds
Apple slices
Toasted Pita chips or French
    bread slices

Preheat the oven to 350 degrees. Cook the bacon in a large skillet over medium heat for 7 minutes or until almost crisp, stirring frequently. Drain excess drippings from the skillet. Add the garlic. Cook for 3 minutes or until the bacon is crisp, stirring frequently. Remove from the heat; set aside.

Beat the cream cheese in a mixing bowl until smooth. Add the half-and-half and mix well. Stir in the bacon mixture, blue cheese and chives. Spoon into a 2-cup baking dish and cover with foil. Bake for 30 minutes or until heated through. Sprinkle with the almonds. Serve with apple slices and toasted pita chips.

Yield: 6 to 8 servings

Blue Cheese Puffs

16 ounces cream cheese, softened
1 cup mayonnaise
4 ounces blue cheese, crumbled
1/4 cup minced fresh chives
1 tablespoon minced fresh onion
1/2 teaspoon cayenne pepper, or
    to taste
1 loaf thinly sliced bread (white,
    whole wheat or a combination)
Paprika

Combine the cream cheese and mayonnaise in a medium bowl and mix well. Stir in the blue cheese, chives, onion and cayenne pepper.

Cut the bread slices with a 1½-inch cookie cutter. Top each bread cutout with 1 tablespoonful of the cheese mixture. Place on a baking sheet; cover with plastic wrap and freeze.

Preheat the oven to 350 degrees. Bake the puffs, uncovered, for 15 minutes or until puffed and lightly browned. Sprinkle with paprika. Serve hot.

Yield: 16 to 20 servings

Nutty Napoleons

96 perfect pecan halves
    (about 5 ounces)
3 ounces cream cheese, softened
2 ounces Stilton cheese, at room
    temperature
2 teaspoons port
1/2 teaspoon honey
Freshly cracked pepper
2 tablespoons chopped fresh chives
    for garnish

Preheat the oven to 350 degrees. Place the pecan halves on a baking sheet. Bake for 7 to 10 minutes or until browned and aromatic; cool.

Combine the cream cheese, Stilton cheese, port, honey and pepper in a food processor and process until smooth. Spoon the cheese mixture into a sealable plastic bag, squeezing into 1 corner.

Place 48 of the pecan halves flat side down on a baking sheet. Cut a small tip off the corner of the plastic bag. Pipe the cheese mixture evenly onto each pecan half. Top with the remaining pecan halves, flat side down. Pipe about 1/4 teaspoon of the remaining cheese mixture on top of each napoleon. Arrange on a serving plate. Garnish with the chives.

Photo on page 18.

Yield: 4 dozen napoleons

Cream Cheese and Feta Spread

16 ounces cream cheese, softened
16 ounces feta cheese
2 tablespoons butter, softened
2 tablespoons white wine
2 teaspoons minced garlic
2 cups sun-dried tomatoes, minced
1 cup pine nuts, toasted
1 cup chopped green onions
Sea salt bagel chips or crackers

Combine the cream cheese, feta cheese, butter, wine and garlic in a food processor and process until smooth. Spoon into an 8-inch serving dish. Chill, covered, for at least 2 hours.

Sprinkle with the sun-dried tomatoes, pine nuts and green onions just before serving. Serve with bagel chips.

Yield: 30 to 50 servings

Mexican Cheesecake

Go to the flower market and pick up several geraniums of the same color. Repot them in small terra cotta pots and arrange them in a line down your table. You can place votive candles between them or in front of them. This is great for an outdoor party. When the guests leave, repot them together in a bigger pot and enjoy them for the rest of the summer, or give them as party favors.

1 cup finely crushed tortilla chips
3 tablespoons butter, melted
16 ounces cream cheese, softened
2 eggs
1 cup (4 ounces) shredded
    Colby cheese
1 cup (4 ounces) shredded Monterey
    Jack cheese
2 (4-ounce) cans diced green
    chiles, drained
1/4 cup chopped jalapeño chiles
1/4 cup sour cream
1/4 cup chopped tomato
1/4 cup chopped black olives
1/4 cup chopped green onions
Savory Tortilla Chips (page 39)

Preheat the oven to 325 degrees. Combine the tortilla chips and butter in a food processor and pulse until mixed. Press onto the bottom of a 9-inch springform pan. Bake for 15 minutes. Remove from the oven; set aside. Maintain the oven temperature.

Beat the cream cheese in a mixing bowl until light and fluffy. Add the eggs 1 at a time, mixing well after each addition. Add the Colby cheese, Monterey Jack cheese, green chiles and jalapeño chiles and mix well. Pour over the crust. Bake for 30 minutes or until the cheesecake tests done. Cool in the pan.

Run a knife around the edge of the cheesecake. Remove the side of the pan. Place the cheesecake on a serving platter. Spread the sour cream over the top. Sprinkle with the tomato, olives and green onions. Serve warm with Savory Tortilla Chips.

Photo on page 21.

Yield: 10 to 12 servings

Chèvre Champignons

2 teaspoons bacon drippings
   or olive oil
1 onion, chopped
1/4 teaspoon kosher salt
Pepper to taste
2 ounces goat cheese,
   at room temperature
2 tablespoons heavy cream
1/4 teaspoon nutmeg
1/8 teaspoon pepper
1 (10-ounce) package frozen
   chopped spinach, thawed
8 ounces bacon, crisp-cooked
   and crumbled
2 tablespoons bacon drippings
   or olive oil
2 (16-ounce) packages large white
   mushrooms, uniform in size,
   stems removed
1/4 teaspoon kosher salt
1/8 teaspoon pepper
2 tablespoons bacon drippings or
   olive oil
1/4 teaspoon kosher salt
1/8 teaspoon pepper

Preheat the oven to 350 degrees. Heat 2 teaspoons bacon drippings in a medium nonstick skillet over medium heat. Add the onion, 1/4 teaspoon salt and pepper to taste. Cook for 5 to 7 minutes or until the onion is tender, stirring constantly. Remove to a medium bowl; cool completely.

Add the goat cheese, cream, nutmeg and 1/8 teaspoon pepper to the onion mixture; stir until well mixed. Drain the spinach, pressing out the excess moisture. Add the spinach and bacon to the cheese mixture and mix well. You may chill the mixture, covered, until ready to use.

Heat 2 tablespoons bacon drippings in a large nonstick skillet over medium heat. Add half the mushrooms. Season with 1/4 teaspoon salt and 1/8 teaspoon pepper. Cook for 4 minutes per side or until golden brown and tender. Place cap side up on a baking sheet lined with paper towels. Wipe out the skillet with a paper towel. Repeat with the remaining 2 tablespoons bacon drippings, mushrooms, 1/4 teaspoon salt and 1/8 teaspoon pepper.

Spoon 1 heaping teaspoonful of the spinach filling into the cavity of each mushroom. Place stuffed side up on a baking sheet. Bake for 5 to 8 minutes or until heated through. Serve warm.

Yield: 3 dozen champignons

1954 - *The Salk vaccine against polio is first administered at the hospital.*

Goat Cheese Crisps

1 cup (4 ounces) finely grated fresh
    Parmesan cheese
8 ounces mild goat cheese
5 tablespoons heavy cream
1 tablespoon finely chopped
    fresh parsley
$1/2$ teaspoon fresh thyme
$1/8$ teaspoon sea salt
Pepper to taste
1 tablespoon chopped fresh chives

Preheat the oven to 325 degrees. Line a baking sheet with a silicone baking mat or parchment paper. Place a $2^1/2$-inch ring mold on the baking sheet. Spoon 1 tablespoonful of the Parmesan cheese into the mold, spreading evenly. Carefully lift the mold straight up, leaving the cheese round intact. Repeat the procedure to make 8 cheese rounds, spacing them at least 1 inch apart. (Do not make more than 8 to prevent them from cooling and hardening before they are shaped.)

Bake for 8 to 10 minutes or until golden. Cool on the baking sheet for 30 seconds. Remove the cheese rounds with a spatula to a clean egg carton, gently pressing each into a separate indentation to form individual cheese cups. Let stand for a few minutes or until firm; remove from the egg carton. Repeat with the remaining Parmesan cheese to make 16 cups.

Combine the goat cheese, cream, parsley, thyme, salt and pepper in a food processor and process until smooth. Spoon into a pastry bag fitted with a medium star tip. Pipe about 1 tablespoonful into each cheese cup. Sprinkle with the chives. Serve immediately.

Note: You may use a plastic egg carton or miniature muffin pan to shape the cheese cups.

Photo on page 15.

Yield: 16 cheese crisps

Tomato and Goat Cheese Crostini

2 large tomatoes, seeded and diced

1 teaspoon olive oil

1/8 teaspoon salt

6 ounces herb-flavored goat
    cheese, crumbled

2 tablespoons chopped fresh basil

1/4 teaspoon pepper

1 (12-ounce) baguette

2 tablespoons olive oil

2 garlic cloves, cut into halves

2 teaspoons chopped fresh parsley

Combine the tomatoes, 1 teaspoon olive oil and salt in a bowl; set aside. Combine the cheese, basil and pepper in a bowl; set aside.

Cut the baguette diagonally into twenty 1/2-inch slices. Brush both sides of the slices with 2 tablespoons olive oil. Grill over medium heat or broil for 2 minutes per side or until golden brown. Rub the cut sides of the garlic cloves over 1 side of each bread slice. Spread evenly with 1/2 tablespoon of the cheese mixture. Top with the tomato mixture and sprinkle with the parsley.

Yield: 20 crostini

Roasted Eggplant Spread

1 eggplant, peeled, cut into
    1-inch pieces

2 red bell peppers, cut into
    1-inch pieces

1 red onion, cut into 1-inch pieces

3 tablespoons olive oil

2 garlic cloves, minced

11/2 teaspoons kosher salt

1/2 teaspoon pepper

1 tablespoon tomato paste

1/2 teaspoon nutmeg

Toasted pita bread or bagel chips

Preheat the oven to 400 degrees. Combine the eggplant, bell peppers, onion, olive oil, garlic, salt and pepper in a large bowl and mix well. Spread on a baking sheet. Roast for 45 minutes or until the vegetables are tender, stirring once. Cool slightly.

Combine the roasted vegetables, tomato paste and nutmeg in a food processor and pulse 3 or 4 times to mix. Season with additional salt and pepper, if desired. Serve with toasted pita bread or bagel chips.

Yield: 6 to 8 servings

Green and Red Pepper Jelly Spread

2 cups (8 ounces) shredded sharp
    Cheddar cheese
2 cups chopped pecans
2 cups chopped green onions
4 to 6 tablespoons mayonnaise-type
    salad dressing
$^1/_2$ cup green pepper jelly
$^1/_2$ cup red pepper jelly
Large thin wheat crackers

Combine the cheese, pecans, green onions and salad dressing in a bowl and mix well. (May be prepared a day in advance. Chill, covered, until ready to serve.)

Mound the cheese mixture in the center of a small, oblong serving dish, about 5×10 inches. Spoon the pepper jelly on either side of the cheese mixture. Serve with crackers.

Yield: 10 to 12 servings

For a festive fall table, drop a container of mums into a hollowed-out pumpkin. Tie a few strands of raffia around the pumpkin and place in the center of the table. Go outside and pick some pretty fall leaves and place underneath the pumpkin so that the colors are visible. This also makes a great, inexpensive hostess gift!

Vidalia Onion Spread

2 cups chopped Vidalia onions
2 cups (8 ounces) shredded
    mozzarella cheese
1 cup mayonnaise
$^1/_2$ cup sour cream
$^1/_2$ cup (2 ounces) shredded
    Parmesan cheese
Dash of Tabasco sauce
Water crackers

Preheat the oven to 375 degrees. Combine the onions, mozzarella cheese, mayonnaise, sour cream, Parmesan cheese and Tabasco sauce in a bowl and mix well. Spoon into a buttered 8×8-inch baking dish. Bake for 30 minutes or until the top and edges are lightly browned. Serve with crackers.

Note: Add a little color to this dish by stirring 2 tablespoons diced pimentos into the cheese mixture before baking.

Yield: 8 servings

1961 - *Dr. Mildred T. Stahlman founds Division of Neonatology at Vanderbilt University Hospital, developing the first respirator for infants with damaged lungs.*

 25

1962 - The Junior League of Nashville Home for Crippled Children becomes an accredited hospital.

Tomato and Onion Tart

3 ripe, firm tomatoes, very thinly
sliced (8 to 10 ounces)
1 (17-ounce) package frozen
puff pastry
1 cup (4 ounces) shredded
mozzarella cheese
$^{1}/_{4}$ cup freshly grated
Parmesan cheese
1$^{1}/_{2}$ tablespoons chopped
fresh oregano
1 tablespoon chopped fresh basil
$^{1}/_{2}$ teaspoon coarsely ground garlic
1 small sweet onion, very thinly
sliced and separated into rings
$^{1}/_{4}$ cup freshly grated
Parmesan cheese

Place the tomato slices between paper towels. Let stand for 30 minutes to remove any excess moisture. Thaw the puff pastry sheets at room temperature for 20 to 30 minutes. Preheat the oven to 400 degrees. Unfold 1 sheet of dough and place on an ungreased heavy baking sheet or baking stone; flatten the dough slightly. Place the second sheet of dough over the first, rotating a half turn so the 2 sheets are offset; flatten the dough slightly.

Layer the mozzarella cheese, $^{1}/_{4}$ cup Parmesan cheese, oregano, basil and garlic over the dough, leaving a 1-inch border. Arrange the tomato slices in slightly overlapping concentric circles over the cheeses. Scatter the onion rings over the tomatoes; sprinkle with $^{1}/_{4}$ cup Parmesan cheese. Fold the edge of the dough carefully, forming a rim around the tart. Bake for 25 to 35 minutes. Cut with a sharp knife or pizza cutter into wedges. Serve immediately.

A *bowl of green apples, green grapes, and sprigs of boxwood looks bright, fresh, and festive on a kitchen table. The various shades of green make a statement and exclude the need for flowers*!

Photo on page 26.

Yield: 8 to 10 servings

1962 - Dr. Mildred T. Stahlman founds nation's first Neonatal Intensive Care Unit at Vanderbilt University Hospital.

27

Spinach Dip with Pita Chips

At your next party, serve a vegetable tray with pizzazz! Thoroughly wash a head of red cabbage. Take a sharp paring knife and hollow the middle, then pour your dip in the cabbage. If there is room, you can always put the dip in a small glass bowl. Fold back some of the outer leaves for a beautiful, yet different, dip container. You can also do the same things with red, green, or yellow peppers. Just hollow them out and pour in the dip. You may need to cut small slices off the bottoms so they will stand straight on the platter.

8 ounces cream cheese
8 ounces Monterey Jack cheese, cut into pieces
1 (10-ounce) can diced tomatoes with green chiles
1 (10-ounce) package frozen chopped spinach, thawed and well drained
1/3 cup shredded Parmesan cheese
1/4 cup diced red onion
2 tablespoons chopped jalapeño chiles
Pita Chips (below)

Preheat the oven to 350 degrees. Heat the cream cheese and Monterey Jack cheese in a saucepan over low heat until melted and smooth, stirring constantly. Add the tomatoes, spinach, Parmesan cheese, onion and jalapeño chiles and mix well. Pour into a shallow 8×8-inch baking pan. Bake for 20 minutes. Serve warm with Pita Chips.

Yield: 6 to 8 servings

Pita Chips

6 pita breads, split horizontally
2 tablespoons butter, melted
1/2 teaspoon cumin
1/2 teaspoon lemon pepper

Preheat the oven to 350 degrees. Brush 1 side of each pita bread half with the butter. Sprinkle evenly with the cumin and lemon pepper. Place buttered side up on a baking sheet. Bake for 20 minutes; cool. Break into pieces for dipping.

Dr. David T. Karzon, *internationally recognized specialist in viral immunology and viral* **1968 -** *infections, joins the staff of Vanderbilt Medical Center as chief of pediatrics and medical director of the future Children's Regional Medical Center.*

Spicy Egg Rolls with Creamy Cilantro Dipping Sauce

1 (5-ounce) package Spanish
    rice mix
1 teaspoon salt
1 pound bulk spicy pork sausage
1 (15-ounce) can black beans,
    rinsed and drained
1 (14-ounce) can petite diced
    tomatoes with green chiles
2 cups (8 ounces) shredded
    Monterey Jack cheese
6 green onions, finely chopped
1 envelope taco seasoning mix
28 egg roll wrappers
1 egg, lightly beaten
1 quart peanut oil for deep-frying
Creamy Cilantro Dipping
    Sauce (below)
Fresh cilantro sprigs for garnish

Cook the rice mix with the salt according to the package directions. Cool completely. Brown the sausage in a skillet over medium heat, stirring until crumbly; drain. Cool completely.

Mix the rice, sausage, beans, tomatoes, cheese, green onions and taco seasoning mix in a large bowl. Spoon about $1/3$ cup of the rice mixture onto the center of each egg roll wrapper. Fold the top corner of the wrapper over the filling, tucking the tip under the filling; fold the left and right corners over the filling. Brush the remaining corner with the egg; tightly roll the filled end toward the remaining corner and press gently to seal.

Heat the peanut oil to 375 degrees in a heavy Dutch oven. Deep-fry the egg rolls in batches in the oil for 2 to 3 minutes or until golden brown. Drain on a wire rack over paper towels. Serve with Creamy Cilantro Dipping Sauce. Garnish with cilantro sprigs.

Yield: 28 egg rolls

Creamy Cilantro Dipping Sauce

2 (10-ounce) cans Mexican-style
    diced tomatoes
2 cups loosely packed fresh cilantro
    leaves (about 1 bunch)
8 ounces cream cheese, softened
1 cup sour cream
3 garlic cloves, minced
Fresh cilantro leaves, finely chopped

Process the tomatoes, cilantro, cream cheese, sour cream and garlic in a food processor until smooth. Spoon into a serving dish. Sprinkle with the cilantro.

Note: For a beautiful presentation, cut the top from a large red bell pepper. Remove the seeds and membrane, leaving the pepper intact. Place the pepper on a serving plate and fill with the dipping sauce.

1970 - A cardiology laboratory is funded by a Given Foundation grant.

29

Reuben Dip

8 ounces cream cheese, softened,
cut into pieces
1/2 cup sour cream
2 tablespoons spicy brown mustard
1 tablespoon ketchup
2 teaspoons finely chopped onion
8 ounces corned beef, chopped
1 cup (4 ounces) shredded
Swiss cheese
1 cup chopped sauerkraut
Rye crackers or sliced party rye or
pimpernickel bread

Preheat the oven to 375 degrees. Combine the cream cheese and sour cream in a food processor and process until smooth. Add the spicy brown mustard, ketchup and onion and process until blended. Add the corned beef, Swiss cheese and sauerkraut and pulse to mix.

Spoon into a 9-inch pie plate. Bake, covered, for 30 minutes. Bake, uncovered, for 5 minutes longer. Serve with rye crackers or sliced party rye or pumpernickel bread.

Yield: 10 to 12 servings

Chicken Salad in Cucumber Cups

2 cups minced cooked chicken
1/2 cup minced celery
1/3 cup mayonnaise
5/8 teaspoon salt
1/2 teaspoon poultry seasoning
4 cucumbers
Dried cranberries for garnish
Celery leaf sprigs for garnish

Combine the chicken, celery, mayonnaise, salt and poultry seasoning in a bowl and mix well. Refrigerate, covered, until chilled.

Remove vertical strips of peel from the cucumbers, making a striped pattern. Cut the cucumbers crosswise into 1-inch slices. Hollow out 1 end of each slice to a 1/2-inch depth, forming a cup. Spoon a generous teaspoonful of chicken salad into each cucumber cup. Garnish each with a dried cranberry and a celery leaf sprig.

Photo on page 15.

Yield: 20 to 24 cucumber cups

1970 - A portion of the Children's Regional Medical Center is redesigned to incorporate the Junior League Home for Crippled Children.

Creamy Deviled Eggs

12 hard-cooked eggs, peeled
8 ounces cream cheese, softened
Dash of cayenne pepper
Salt and freshly ground black
   pepper to taste
Paprika to taste
Pickle juice to taste
Caviar, caper, or crumbled cooked
   bacon for garnish
Paprika, chopped fresh parsley or
   chopped fresh dillweed
   for garnish

Cut the eggs crosswise into halves, creating round rather than oblong shapes. Cut a small piece off the rounded ends so the eggs will stand upright. Remove the yolks to a food processor.

Add the cream cheese, cayenne pepper, salt, black pepper, paprika and pickle juice to the food processor and process until smooth and creamy. Adjust the seasonings.

Spoon the egg yolk mixture into a pastry bag fitted with a round tip. Pipe into the egg whites. Garnish with caviar and paprika. Chill, covered, until ready to serve.

Note: This version is creamier than most and is wonderful served with the slightly crunchy textured toppings. Round deviled eggs make a pretty presentation and are much easier to pick up and eat than oblong deviled eggs.

Photo on page 32.

Yield: 2 dozen deviled eggs

Having trouble peeling hard-boiled eggs? Tap them gently along the middle of the egg and then roll back and forth with the palm of your hand. This loosens the membrane, allowing it to peel easily.

1970 - *Dr. David T. Karzon creates "hospital within a hospital" concept and establishes various centers within the main hospital that specialize in pediatric services.*

31

Smoked Salmon and Egg Salad

1/4 cup mayonnaise

1/4 cup sour cream

1 teaspoon lemon juice

1/4 teaspoon pepper

1/8 teaspoon salt

6 hard-cooked eggs, chopped

4 ounces smoked salmon,
    finely chopped

1/2 cup minced red onion

1 tablespoon minced fresh dillweed

1 to 2 teaspoons drained capers

Toasted bagels, crackers or sliced
    party pumpernickel bread

Combine the mayonnaise, sour cream, lemon juice, pepper and salt in a large bowl and mix well. Fold in the eggs, salmon, onion, dillweed and capers. Serve with toasted bagels.

Yield: 6 to 8 servings

Smoked Trout Mousse on Endive

6 to 8 endive

8 ounces cream cheese, softened

4 ounces soft goat cheese (chèvre)

1/4 cup chopped scallions

3 tablespoons snipped
    fresh dillweed

2 tablespoons snipped fresh
    flat-leaf parsley

8 ounces smoked trout fillets,
    skinned, boned and flaked

Fresh dillweed sprigs for garnish

Rinse the endive and separate into individual leaves. Pat dry with paper towels; chill. Beat the cream cheese and goat cheese at medium speed in a medium mixing bowl until smooth. Stir in the scallions, 3 tablespoons dillweed and parsley. Fold in the trout. Chill, covered, for 2 to 6 hours.

Spoon the trout mixture onto the endive leaves. Garnish with fresh dillweed sprigs.

Note: You may substitute three 8-inch-long cucumbers for the endive. Cut the cucumbers into 1/2-inch-thick slices.

Photo on page 32.

Yield: 12 to 15 servings

Salmon and Hearts of Palm Rolls

8 ounces cream cheese, softened

1/2 cup loosely packed chopped
fresh dillweed

1/4 teaspoon kosher salt

10 (3×4 inch) thin slices lox or
smoked salmon

1 (14-ounce) can hearts of palm,
rinsed and drained

Fresh dillweed sprigs, chive sprigs,
cracked pepper or caviar
for garnish

Photo on page 32.

Beat the cream cheese, dillweed and salt in a mixing bowl until smooth.

Place the salmon slices in a single layer on a work surface. Spread each slice with about 1 tablespoonful of the cheese mixture, dividing it evenly. Pat the hearts of palm dry. Place 1 heart of palm at 1 end of each salmon slice and roll as for a jelly roll, enclosing the heart of palm. Place the rolls in an airtight container. Chill for at least 1 hour. (May be prepared up to 1 day in advance.)

Cut the chilled rolls crosswise into 1/2- to 1-inch slices, creating pinwheels. Garnish with fresh dillweed sprigs.

Note: You may substitute chilled steamed asparagus spears for the hearts of palm.

Yield: 30 rolls

1970 - *Nashville Tri Delta Alumnae Chapter creates Eve of Janus presentation ball to benefit the Hematology/Oncology Clinic.*

Cold Crab Salad

1 medium or large onion,
   finely chopped
1 pound fresh lump crab
   meat, rinsed
Salt and pepper to taste
1/2 cup vegetable oil
1/2 cup cider vinegar
1/2 cup ice water
Crackers or lettuce cups

Layer half the onion, the crab meat and the remaining onion in a 1 1/2-quart glass dish or trifle dish. Sprinkle with salt and pepper. Pour the oil, vinegar and water over the top. Marinate, covered, in the refrigerator for 2 days. When ready to serve, drain off any excess liquid. Serve with crackers or in lettuce cups. Or, just stand in the door of the refrigerator and spoon it into your mouth—it's that good!

Yield: 6 servings

A single floating flower, especially fragrant ones like gardenias and magnolias, can be a very simple, yet elegant, table arrangement. One floating flower surrounded by tea lights can add the perfect touch to a dinner table. Keeping flowers and candles low gives a more intimate feeling to the setting.

Creamy Hot Crab Dip

1 (8-ounce) can crab meat, rinsed,
   drained and flaked
8 ounces cream cheese, softened
2 tablespoons milk
1 tablespoon finely chopped onion
1 teaspoon horseradish
Salt and pepper to taste
Slivered almonds
Paprika

Combine the crab meat, cream cheese, milk, onion, horseradish, salt and pepper in a bowl and mix well. Spoon into a lightly greased microwave-safe pie plate, spreading evenly. Sprinkle with almonds and paprika. Microwave on High for about 5 minutes or bake in a preheated 350-degree oven for 15 minutes. Serve with small round party crackers.

Yield: 6 to 8 servings

1971 - *Community women approach Dr. Karzon about forming a support group of volunteers to raise funds, create public awareness of the hospital, and enhance non-medical aspects at the hospital.*

 35

Eastern Shore Crab Cakes

1¹/2 tablespoons soybean oil

¹/2 cup minced celery

¹/2 cup minced onion

1 pound lump crab meat

¹/3 cup saltine crumbs

¹/3 cup mayonnaise

1 egg, beaten

2 tablespoons Dijon mustard

1¹/2 tablespoons Old Bay seasoning

Pepper to taste

1 cup saltine crumbs

1 tablespoon vegetable oil

1 tablespoon butter

Red Pepper Rémoulade
    Sauce (below)

Photo on page 37.

Heat the soybean oil in a sauté pan over medium heat. Add the celery and onion and cook until tender, but not browned, stirring frequently; cool. Combine the crab meat, ¹/3 cup cracker crumbs, mayonnaise, egg, Dijon mustard, Old Bay seasoning and pepper in a bowl and mix well. Fold in the cooled celery and onion.

Place 1 cup cracker crumbs in a shallow dish. Drop 2-ounce portions of the crab mixture into the cracker crumbs and roll to coat. Shape into ³/4-inch-thick round cakes. Place on a baking sheet lined with parchment paper or plastic wrap. Chill, securely wrapped, for 30 minutes or until ready to cook.

Preheat the oven to 350 degrees. Heat the vegetable oil and butter in an ovenproof sauté pan. Fry the crab cakes in batches in the oil mixture for 1 minute per side. Place the pan in the oven. Bake for 5 minutes. Serve with Red Pepper Rémoulade Sauce.

Yield: 12 (2-ounce) cakes

Red Pepper Rémoulade Sauce

4 cups mayonnaise

1 (16-ounce) can roasted red
    peppers, drained and minced

¹/4 cup minced fresh parsley

¹/4 cup minced fresh tarragon

¹/4 cup drained capers, minced

¹/4 cup minced cornichons

2 tablespoons minced shallot

Combine the mayonnaise, roasted red peppers, parsley, tarragon, capers, cornichons and shallot in a bowl and mix well. Refrigerate in an airtight container and chill before serving.

Chef Ray's Tropical Rock Shrimp Salsa

1 pound rock shrimp, peeled

1 (13-ounce) can coconut milk

2 mangoes, peeled and chopped

1/2 red onion, chopped

3 bananas, chopped

1 ripe tomato, chopped

1 poblano chile, peeled, seeded
    and chopped

1 cup fresh lime juice

1/2 cup olive oil

2 tablespoons grated coconut

1 tablespoon chopped fresh cilantro

2 teaspoons sea salt

1 tablespoon freshly minced garlic

3 scallions, thinly sliced

Poach the shrimp in the coconut milk. Remove the shrimp with a slotted spoon to a bowl. Refrigerate, covered, until chilled.

Combine the shrimp, mangoes, onion, bananas, tomato and poblano chile in a bowl and mix well; set aside.

Combine the lime juice, olive oil, coconut, cilantro, salt and garlic in a bowl and mix well. Pour over the shrimp mixture. Chill, covered, for 2 hours. Sprinkle with the scallions before serving. Serve with corn tortillas.

Note: For enhanced flavor, chill the salsa for 24 hours.

Yield: 10 to 12 servings

Marinated Shrimp

2 pounds shrimp, boiled, peeled
    and deveined

1 to 2 (12-ounce) bottles
    Champagne salad dressing

12 to 14 bay leaves

2 tablespoons sesame seeds

Photo on page 18.

Place the shrimp in a large sealable plastic bag. Add the salad dressing, bay leaves and sesame seeds; seal the bag and shake to mix. Marinate in the refrigerator for at least 3 hours.

Drain the shrimp, discarding the marinade. Place the shrimp in a serving dish and serve with wooden picks.

Note: After boiling shrimp, simply serve with a cocktail sauce. Leave tails on and serve in elegant glasses.

Yield: 6 to 8 servings

Savory Tortilla Chips

1/3 cup grated Parmesan cheese

7 tablespoons sesame seeds

1 tablespoon poppy seeds

1/4 teaspoon sweet paprika

Pinch of salt

Pinch of pepper

6 flour tortillas

6 tablespoons butter, melted

Ben's Favorite Dip (below) or
    Mexican Cheesecake (page 20)

Photo on page 21.

Preheat the oven to 400 degrees. Combine the cheese, sesame seeds, poppy seeds, paprika, salt and pepper in a bowl and mix well. Place the tortillas on a cutting board. Brush with the butter. Sprinkle evenly with the cheese mixture. Cut each tortilla into 8 wedges. Place on a baking sheet lined with foil.

Bake for 8 minutes or until golden brown. Remove to a wire rack; cool. Serve with Ben's Favorite Dip.

Yield: 4 dozen chips

Ben's Favorite Dip

1 (16-ounce) package frozen
    supersweet corn

2 tablespoons butter

Salt and pepper to taste

1 cup chopped onion

1/2 cup chopped red bell pepper

1/3 cup chopped green onions

1 teaspoon minced garlic

1 (4-ounce) can chopped
    green chiles

2 cups (8 ounces) shredded
    Monterey Jack cheese

3/4 cup mayonnaise

Preheat the oven to 350 degrees. Sauté the corn in 1 tablespoon of the butter in a skillet until lightly browned and caramelized. Season with salt and pepper. Remove to a bowl.

Add the remaining 1 tablespoon butter to the skillet. Sauté the onion, bell pepper, green onions and garlic in the butter. Stir in the green chiles. Cook for 5 minutes.

Stir the onion mixture, cheese and mayonnaise into the corn mixture and mix well. Spoon into an 8×8-inch baking dish. Bake for 20 to 30 minutes or until golden brown and bubbly.

Yield: 6 servings

Salads & Soups

chapter two

Chandler's Party Salad

Saffire's Ribbon Salad

Italian Party Salad

Fall Salad with Maple Mustard Vinaigrette

Seasonal Mixed Greens Salad

with Sesame Dressing

Will's Favorite Salad

Avocado with Warm Tomato and

Basil Vinaigrette

Baked Spinach Salad

Broccoli Floret Salad

Pasta and Seafood Salad with Basil

Overton's Lime JELL-O Salad

Gazpacho

Basantes' Butternut Squash Soup

Autumn Bisque

Curried Cream of Chicken Soup

Tortilla Soup

Minestrone from Basantes

Country Soup Supper

White Bean Soup

Italian Onion Soup

Butternut Lobster Bisque

Mario's Seafood Soup

Chandler's Party Salad

BLUE CHEESE SALAD DRESSING

Combine 1 cup sour cream, 1/4 cup buttermilk, 4 ounces crumbled blue cheese, 2 teaspoons minced fresh parsley, 1 teaspoon Worcestershire sauce, 1/2 teaspoon freshly minced garlic, and salt and pepper to taste in a jar. Cover and shake until well mixed.

DRESSING

1/2 cup poppy seed salad dressing

1 teaspoon grated orange zest

1 tablespoon orange juice

SALAD

1 pound asparagus spears, trimmed

2 tablespoons water

*6 to 8 cups torn spring mix
    and/or romaine*

1 cup sliced strawberries

1 cup blueberries

2 small or 1 medium star fruit, sliced

*12 to 16 ounces cooked turkey,
    cut into 1/2-inch cubes*

1/4 cup pecan halves

Sunflower seeds

*1 teaspoon grated orange zest or
    lemon zest for garnish*

Photo on page 43.

For the dressing, whisk the salad dressing, orange zest and orange juice in a bowl; set aside.

For the salad, cut the asparagus into 1-inch pieces. Place in a microwave-safe dish with the water. Microwave, covered, on High for 5 minutes; drain. Rinse with cold water. Let stand in a bowl of cold water until cool; drain.

Combine the asparagus, spring mix, strawberries, blueberries, star fruit and turkey in a bowl; toss to mix. Add the pecan halves and sunflower seeds.

Pour the dressing over the salad and toss lightly. Garnish with orange zest.

Yield: 4 to 6 servings

1971 - *The infectious diseases department is established.*

Saffire's Ribbon Salad

WHITE PEACH VINAIGRETTE

White peaches, peeled

1/4 cup orange juice concentrate

3 tablespoons rice wine vinegar

1 shallot, chopped

1 teaspoon kosher salt

Pinch of freshly ground pepper

3/4 cup canola oil

1/4 cup olive oil

SPICY FRIED WALNUTS

2 cups walnut halves

2 quarts water

3 cups confectioners' sugar

1/4 teaspoon cayenne pepper

Vegetable oil for deep-frying

RIBBON SALAD

1 head iceberg lettuce

1 cup Spicy Fried Walnuts

3/4 cup White Peach Vinaigrette,
*   or to taste*

1/2 cup crumbled blue cheese

1 teaspoon kosher salt

Dash of freshly ground pepper

1 (7-ounce) bag vegetable chips

For the vinaigrette, purée enough peaches in a blender to make 1/4 cup purée. Add the orange juice concentrate, vinegar, shallot, salt and pepper to the blender and process until smooth. Add the canola oil and olive oil in a fine stream, processing constantly at high speed until smooth; set aside.

For the walnuts, combine the walnuts and water in a saucepan. Bring to a full rolling boil. Boil for 10 minutes; drain. Combine the confectioners' sugar and cayenne pepper in a bowl and mix well. Add the walnuts and toss to coat. Heat the oil to 350 degrees in a deep fryer. Add the walnuts. Deep-fry for 4 to 5 minutes. Remove to a paper towel-lined baking sheet; cool.

For the salad, chill 4 salad plates and forks in the refrigerator. Cut the lettuce into halves. Cut each half into 1/4-inch slices. Combine the lettuce, walnuts, vinaigrette, blue cheese, salt and pepper in a bowl and toss to mix. Divide evenly among the chilled salad plates. Top with the vegetable chips. Serve immediately.

Yield: 4 servings

1972 - *Playroom expansions are completed.*

Italian Party Salad

DRESSING

1/2 cup olive oil

1/2 cup wine vinegar

1 1/2 tablespoons chopped fresh oregano

1 tablespoon minced garlic

1 teaspoon salt

1 teaspoon pepper

SALAD

1 (32-ounce) bag mixed salad greens

1 (16-ounce) can pitted black olives, drained

1 (16-ounce) can quartered artichoke hearts, drained and cut into halves

1 (15-ounce) can chick-peas, drained

1 cup grape tomatoes (optional)

1/2 red onion, chopped

For the dressing, whisk the olive oil, vinegar, oregano, garlic, salt and pepper in a bowl; set aside.

For the salad, combine the salad greens, olives, artichokes, chick-peas, tomatoes and onion in a bowl; toss to mix. Pour the dressing over the salad and toss to coat.

Yield: 8 servings

Don't have a salad spinner, but your lettuce is wet? Use a plastic grocery bag lined with several layers of paper toweling as a substitute. Put lettuce into the bag, gather the top, and shake it. The greens will be perfectly dry and ready for your favorite dressing.

Fall Salad with
Maple Mustard Vinaigrette

Nothing tastes better or looks prettier than a crisp beautiful salad. Try to live on the edge once in a while and use some red or green leaf lettuce instead of iceberg.

SPICED PECANS

1 tablespoon brown sugar
2 teaspoons olive oil
1/2 teaspoon cayenne pepper
1/4 teaspoon salt
1/4 teaspoon cumin
1 cup pecan halves

MAPLE MUSTARD VINAIGRETTE

1/2 cup extra-virgin olive oil
1/4 cup maple syrup
2 small shallots, minced
4 teaspoons fresh lemon juice
1 teaspoon salt
1 teaspoon freshly ground pepper
1 teaspoon Dijon mustard

SALAD

8 cups mesclun
*2 firm ripe Bartlett pears, cut into
    1/4-inch slices*
*1 cup seedless red grapes, cut
    into halves*
1 cup thinly sliced red onion
3/4 cup Maple Mustard Vinaigrette
*4 ounces Roquefort cheese, chilled
    and crumbled*
1 cup Spiced Pecans
Freshly ground pepper to taste

For the pecans, preheat the oven to 350 degrees. Combine the brown sugar, olive oil, cayenne pepper, salt and cumin in a bowl and mix well. Add the pecans and toss to completely coat. Spoon the pecans onto a baking sheet. Bake for 12 to 15 minutes or until lightly browned, stirring after 6 minutes. Cool on the baking sheet.

For the vinaigrette, whisk the olive oil, maple syrup, shallots, lemon juice, salt, pepper and Dijon mustard in a medium bowl; set aside.

For the salad, combine the mesclun, pears, grapes and onion in a large bowl. Add the vinaigrette and toss to mix. Divide evenly among 6 salad plates. Top with cheese and pecans. Season with pepper.

Yield: 6 servings

Seasonal Mixed Greens Salad with Sesame Dressing

SESAME DRESSING

1/2 cup rice vinegar

1/4 cup honey

1/4 cup olive oil

Freshly minced garlic to taste

Salt and freshly ground pepper
   to taste

2 tablespoons sesame seeds, toasted

SEASONAL MIXED GREENS

Mesclun, spinach, Bibb lettuce,
   romaine, leaf lettuce, arugula

SEASONAL TOPPINGS

Spring: Baby carrots, spring onions,
   fresh mozzarella slices, cherry
   tomatoes, slivered almonds

Summer: Fresh berries, peach
   slices, crumbled goat cheese,
   homegrown tomatoes

Fall: Crisp pear slices, tart apple
   slices, crumbled blue cheese,
   sugared pecans

Winter: Grapes, orange slices, dried
   cranberries, red onion slices,
   toasted pecans

For the dressing, whisk the vinegar, honey, olive oil, garlic, salt and pepper in a glass bowl. Add the sesame seeds and whisk until emulsified. Chill in a covered jar or bottle until ready to use. Shake well before serving.

For the salad, use any combination of seasonal mixed greens as a salad base, choosing from those listed or whatever is in season. Top the greens with any of the seasonal toppings listed and the desired amount of dressing and toss to mix.

Note: It's easy to prepare sugared pecans. Melt 1 cup butter and 4 cups packed brown sugar in a saucepan. Bring to a boil, stirring constantly. Add 1 teaspoon ground cinnamon and 4 cups pecan halves and mix well. Spread the pecans on a sheet of parchment paper. Let stand until cool; sugar coating will harden. Store in an airtight container until ready to use.

Yield: 6 servings

Photo on page 41.

HONEY MUSTARD DRESSING

Combine 3/4 cup mayonnaise, 3 tablespoons honey, 3 tablespoons prepared mustard, 1 tablespoon lemon juice and salt and pepper to taste in a bowl. Whisk until well mixed.

Will's Favorite Salad

8 cups mixed salad greens

1 (14-ounce) can mandarin
    oranges, drained

1 (8-ounce) package chopped dates

1 small red onion, thinly sliced

1/4 cup vegetable oil

2 tablespoons lemon juice

1 teaspoon salt

1 teaspoon Worcestershire sauce

1/4 teaspoon pepper

1 cup crumbled feta cheese

Combine the salad greens, mandarin oranges, dates and onion in a large bowl. Whisk the oil, lemon juice, salt, Worcestershire sauce and pepper in a bowl. Pour the dressing over the salad and toss. Sprinkle the cheese over the top. Serve immediately.

Note: Salad and dressing may be prepared in advance. Cover and chill separately. Toss together and sprinkle with the cheese just before serving.

Yield: 6 servings

Avocado with Warm Tomato and Basil Vinaigrette

2 large ripe tomatoes, peeled,
    seeded and diced

1/2 cup fresh basil leaves, chopped

1/2 cup light olive oil

1/4 cup red wine vinegar

2 tablespoons Dijon mustard

Salt and pepper to taste

2 avocados, cut into halves, pitted
    and peeled

4 fresh basil leaves for garnish

Combine the tomatoes, chopped basil, olive oil, vinegar, Dijon mustard, salt and pepper in a saucepan. Bring to a simmer, stirring occasionally; remove from the heat.

Place the avocado halves on individual plates. Spoon the warm tomato dressing over the avocados. Garnish each with a basil leaf. Serve immediately.

Yield: 4 servings

Photo on page 49.

Baked Spinach Salad

DRESSING
1¼ cups sesame oil
1 cup vegetable oil
½ cup honey
½ cup rice vinegar
¼ cup sesame seeds, toasted
¼ cup minced shallots
¼ cup lime juice
1 tablespoon minced
   fresh gingerroot

SALAD
1 (6-ounce) bag curly spinach
Salt and white pepper to taste
½ cup sliced shiitake mushrooms
¼ cup shredded Swiss cheese

For the dressing, whisk the sesame oil, vegetable oil, honey, vinegar, sesame seeds, shallots, lime juice and gingerroot in a bowl.

For the salad, preheat the oven to 400 degrees. Place the spinach in a bowl; season with salt and white pepper. Add the mushrooms and ½ cup of the dressing and toss to mix. Divide evenly between 2 ovenproof salad plates; sprinkle with the cheese. Bake for 1 minute.

Note: Cover and refrigerate the remaining dressing for up to 1 week. Or double the salad ingredients and use all the dressing for 4 servings.

Yield: 2 servings

Broccoli Floret Salad

¾ cup mayonnaise
¼ cup sugar
2 tablespoons vinegar
4 cups broccoli florets, cut into
   bite-size pieces
¼ cup raisins
¼ cup chopped red onion
8 slices bacon, crisp-cooked
   and crumbled

Combine the mayonnaise, sugar and vinegar in a bowl and mix well. Refrigerate, covered, until chilled.

Toss the broccoli, raisins and onion in a large bowl. Top with the bacon. Pour the dressing over the salad just before serving.

Note: The dressing may be made ahead and refrigerated; do not pour over the salad until ready to serve.

Yield: 6 to 8 servings

Pasta and Seafood Salad with Basil

Salt to taste

1 pound fresh medium shrimp,
    peeled and deveined

1 pound bay scallops, rinsed

8 ounces pasta

1 cup frozen baby peas, thawed

1/2 cup chopped red bell pepper

1/2 cup minced red onion

1/2 cup olive oil

3 to 4 tablespoons fresh lemon juice

1/2 cup chopped fresh basil

Pepper to taste

1 cup black olives

Bring enough salted water to cover the shrimp to a boil in a stockpot. Add the shrimp and scallops. Cook for 1 minute or until the shrimp turn pink and the scallops are tender; drain immediately. Cook the pasta according to the package directions; drain. Toss the shrimp, scallops and pasta in a large bowl. Add the peas, bell pepper and onion. Combine the olive oil, lemon juice and basil in a bowl; season with salt and pepper. Pour over the shrimp mixture and toss to mix. Refrigerate, covered, until chilled. Bring to room temperature. Stir in the olives just before serving.

Yield: 8 to 10 servings

Overton's Lime JELL-O Salad

1 (3-ounce) package JELL-O Brand
    Lime Flavor Gelatin

1 cup boiling water

1/2 cup cold water

1 (8-ounce) can crushed pineapple,
    drained, or 1 small jar
    maraschino cherries, drained

1 1/2 ounces cream cheese, softened

1 tablespoon mayonnaise

4 ounces whipped topping

1 1/4 cups finely chopped pecans

Dissolve the gelatin in the boiling water in a bowl. Stir in the cold water. Let stand until cool. Stir in the pineapple. Chill just until partially set.

Combine the cream cheese and mayonnaise in a bowl and mix well. Stir in the whipped topping. Add to the gelatin mixture and mix well. Stir in the pecans. Pour into a serving bowl. Chill for 3 to 4 hours or until set.

Yield: 8 servings

Gazpacho

To store fresh picked herbs, tie the stalks together and wrap in a damp paper towel. Herbs can also be placed in a vase with water and put out on the countertop but not in the sunlight.

2 large tomatoes, peeled
    and chopped
1 green bell pepper, chopped
1 cucumber, peeled and chopped
1 onion, chopped
1 (46-ounce) can tomato juice
2 scallions, thinly sliced
1 garlic clove, crushed
2 tablespoons olive oil
2 tablespoons red wine vinegar
2 tablespoons lime juice
1 1/2 tablespoons lemon juice
1 teaspoon tarragon
1 teaspoon basil
1 teaspoon honey
Dash of hot red pepper sauce
1/2 teaspoon salt
1/4 teaspoon pepper
1/4 teaspoon cumin

Combine the tomatoes, bell pepper, cucumber and onion with enough tomato juice to cover in a food processor and pulse until finely chopped; do not purée. Remove to a large container.

Stir in the remaining tomato juice, scallions, garlic, olive oil, vinegar, lime juice, lemon juice, tarragon, basil, honey, pepper sauce, salt, pepper and cumin. Chill, covered, for at least 2 hours or for up to 3 days.

Yield: 9 servings

Basantes' Butternut Squash Soup

1 butternut squash, peeled, cut into
    halves and seeded
Salt and white pepper to taste
4 cups vegetable stock
1 onion, coarsely chopped
1 teaspoon Italian seasoning
1¹/₂ cups heavy cream
1 cup honey
10 fresh basil leaves

Preheat the oven to 350 degrees. Place the butternut squash on a baking sheet; season with salt and white pepper. Roast for 45 minutes or until tender.

Meanwhile, combine the vegetable stock, onion and Italian seasoning in a saucepan. Cook until heated through. Simmer for 20 minutes. Add the roasted squash and cream. Bring to a boil. Simmer briefly. Stir in the honey and basil. Process the soup in batches in a blender or food processor until puréed. Season with salt and white pepper.

Yield: 8 servings

Looking for a different way to serve soup? Hollow out a round loaf of bread and pour in the soup. Use the hollowed-out bread to dip in the soup.

Autumn Bisque

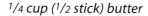

1/4 cup (1/2 stick) butter
3 pounds butternut squash, peeled and cut into 1-inch cubes
3 leeks, white and light green parts only, sliced
3 apples, peeled and chopped
1 tablespoon chopped fresh thyme
3 tablespoons flour
6 cups chicken stock
1 1/2 cups apple cider (not apple juice)
1 tablespoon curry powder
1/2 cup heavy cream
Salt and pepper to taste
Toasted pumpkin seeds for garnish

Photo on page 54.

Heat the butter in a large saucepan over medium-high heat until melted. Add the butternut squash, leeks, apples, thyme and flour. Sauté for 5 to 10 minutes or until the leeks and apples begin to soften, stirring frequently. Stir in the chicken stock, apple cider and curry powder. Bring to a boil. Reduce the heat. Simmer for 30 minutes.

Process the soup in batches in a food processor until smooth. Return to the saucepan. Stir in the cream, salt and pepper. Cook until heated through. Ladle into soup bowls or carved out pumpkin squash and garnish with pumpkin seeds.

Yield: 12 servings

Looking for a unique way to serve raw vegetables? "Plant" carrots, celery sticks, or asparagus in terra cotta pots. Line a terra cotta saucer with foil or place a clear glass bowl in it for the dip.

1974 - *The Child Development Center is established to evaluate children for developmental problems and assist other professionals in making appropriate decisions for the treatment of children.*

 55

Curried Cream of Chicken Soup

BOUQUET GARNI

Place 1 bay leaf, 3 sprigs of thyme, 4 large sprigs of parsley, and one 5-inch celery rib with leaves on one 5-inch piece of the green part of a leek. Cover with another 5-inch piece of the green part of a leek. Tie securely with fine string leaving one length of string attached so that the bouquet garni can be easily removed. See Basic Chicken Stock on page 57.

6 tablespoons butter

2 cups chopped yellow onions

3 carrots, peeled and sliced

1 to 2 ribs celery, sliced

1 1/2 tablespoons curry powder, or to taste

5 cups chicken stock

2 1/2 to 3 pounds chicken pieces, skinned

1/2 cup rice

6 fresh parsley sprigs

1/2 cup half-and-half

1/2 cup heavy cream

Salt and pepper to taste

Melt the butter in a stockpot over low heat. Add the onions, carrots, celery and curry powder. Cook, covered, for 25 minutes or until the vegetables are tender, stirring occasionally.

Add the chicken stock, chicken, rice and parsley. Bring to a boil. Reduce the heat. Simmer, covered, for 45 minutes or until the chicken is cooked through. Cool the chicken in the soup.

Remove the chicken from the soup. Chop the chicken, discarding the bones; set aside.

Strain the soup, reserving the vegetables and rice and discarding the parsley. Combine 1 cup of the soup, half-and-half and heavy cream in the stockpot. Stir in 4 cups of the soup or enough to reach the desired consistency. Stir in the reserved vegetables, rice and chicken. Cook until heated through. Season with salt and pepper. Serve immediately.

Yield: 10 servings

The National Center on Abuse and Neglect awards Vanderbilt Medical School a two-year grant to study motherhood.

Tortilla Soup

4 boneless skinless chicken
    breast halves
1 onion, chopped
1/4 cup (1/2 stick) butter
2 (10-ounce) cans diced tomatoes
    with green chiles
1 (16-ounce) can corn
1 (16-ounce) can black beans,
    rinsed and drained
1 (16-ounce) can tomato sauce
1 (4-ounce) can chopped
    green chiles
1/2 cup chicken stock
2 teaspoons chopped fresh cilantro
1 garlic clove, crushed
1 teaspoon cumin
1 teaspoon chili powder
1/2 teaspoon oregano
1/2 teaspoon pepper
3 dashes of Tabasco sauce
Shredded Monterey Jack cheese
Sour cream
Tortilla chips

Place the chicken in a Dutch oven and add enough water to cover. Bring to a boil. Reduce the heat. Simmer until the chicken is cooked through. Skim the fat from the cooking liquid. Remove the chicken. Let the cooking liquid cool. Dice the chicken; return to the cooking liquid.

Sauté the onion in the butter in a skillet until tender. Add the onion mixture, tomatoes, corn, black beans, tomato sauce, green chiles, chicken stock, cilantro, garlic, cumin, chili powder, oregano, pepper and Tabasco sauce to the chicken mixture. Bring to a boil. Reduce the heat. Simmer until heated through.

Ladle into soup bowls. Top each serving with cheese, sour cream and tortilla chips.

Yield: 6 servings

BASIC CHICKEN STOCK

Heat 1 tablespoon olive oil in a large stockpot over high heat. Add 1 large quartered peeled onion, 1 large chopped peeled carrot, and 2 chopped celery ribs. Sauté for 2 to 3 minutes. Add 1 bulb garlic cut into halves; 1 bouquet garni; 2 pounds uncooked chicken bones; and 4 quarts of cold water. Bring to a boil. Reduce the heat to low and simmer for 2 hours. Skim the surface and strain through a large fine-mesh sieve. Discard the bones and vegetables. This will make 3 quarts of stock. See Bouquet Garni on page 56.

1975 - The Comprehensive Development Evaluation Center opens offering diagnostic and consultative services to patients with complex developmental disabilities.

 57

1975 - *Nashville Tri Delta Alumnae Chapter's Eve of Janus raises $18,000 for the Hematology/Oncology Clinic.*

Minestrone from Basantes

2 ribs celery, chopped

1 onion, chopped

1 large carrot, chopped

1 leek, white and light green parts
    only, sliced

2 tablespoons olive oil

1 teaspoon thyme

1 teaspoon freshly chopped garlic

1 quart free-range chicken stock

2 chicken bouillon cubes

6 boneless skinless chicken breast
    halves, chopped

1 (15-ounce) can organic black beans

1 (15-ounce) can organic pinto beans

$1/2$ cup tomato sauce

6 fresh basil leaves, chopped

6 fresh sage leaves, chopped

Salt and pepper to taste

$1/2$ cup water

$1/4$ cup cornstarch

8 ounces small round pasta

Grated Parmesan cheese

Photo on page 58.

Sauté the celery, onion, carrot and leek in the olive oil in a saucepan. Stir in the thyme. Cook until fragrant, stirring occasionally. Add the garlic. Cook for $1 1/2$ minutes or until the vegetables are tender, stirring constantly. Add the chicken stock and bouillon cubes and cook until the bouillon is dissolved, stirring constantly. Bring to a boil. Reduce the heat to low. Simmer for 5 minutes. Add the chicken. Bring to a boil, stirring occasionally.

Combine half the undrained black beans and half the undrained pinto beans in a food processor and process until smooth. Add the puréed beans, remaining beans, tomato sauce, basil, sage, salt and pepper to the soup. Cook until heated through, stirring constantly. Combine the water and cornstarch in a bowl and mix well. Add the cornstarch mixture gradually to the soup, stirring constantly. Bring to a boil. Cook to desired consistency. Cook the pasta according to the package directions; drain. Stir into the soup. Ladle into soup bowls. Sprinkle each serving with cheese.

Note: For best results, prepare all the ingredients before you begin cooking.

Yield: 4 to 6 servings

Country Soup Supper

If you want to speed up the lengthy process of cooking beans, use a pressure cooker. There is no need to presoak beans, and most types can be cooked to perfection in under 30 minutes. When pressure cooking beans, use beer or stock and an onion and a bay leaf for added flavor.

1 1/2 pounds boneless lean beef
    brisket, chuck or stew meat, cut
    into bite-size pieces
1 quart water
1 teaspoon salt or seasoned salt
    (such as Cavender's
    Greek seasoning)
1/4 teaspoon pepper
1 garlic clove, minced
1 bay leaf
2 ribs celery, chopped (about 1 cup)
2 large carrots, chopped
    (about 1 cup)
1 onion, chopped
1/4 head cabbage, cut into
    1-inch wedges
2 (8-ounce) cans tomato sauce
3 tablespoons quick-cooking
    pearled barley
1 (15-ounce) can red beans or
    kidney beans

Combine the beef, water, salt and pepper in a stockpot or Dutch oven. Bring to a boil; skim the surface. Add the garlic and bay leaf. Reduce the heat. Simmer, covered, for 1 1/2 hours. Remove and discard the bay leaf.

Add the celery, carrots, onion, cabbage, tomato sauce and barley and mix well. Simmer, covered, for 20 minutes. Stir in the undrained beans. Simmer, covered, for 10 minutes or until the vegetables are tender. Ladle into soup bowls. Serve with crusty French bread.

Yield: 6 servings

1976 - Nashville Tri Delta Alumnae Chapter raises $22,000 for the Hematology/Oncology Clinic.

White Bean Soup

1 pound dried, or 4 (15-ounce)
  cans Great Northern beans,
  drained
1 or 2 ham hocks
2¹/2 quarts water
1 onion, chopped
1 rib celery, chopped
1 carrot, chopped
2 bay leaves
2 teaspoons salt
¹/4 teaspoon black pepper
¹/4 teaspoon cayenne pepper,
  or to taste

Sort and rinse the beans. Soak in water to cover for 8 to 10 hours.

Remove and shred the meat from the ham hock. Drain the beans. Bring 2¹/2 quarts water to a boil in a large saucepan. Add the beans, shredded meat and ham hock. Return to a boil. Add the onion, celery, carrot, bay leaves, salt, black pepper and cayenne pepper. Cook over low heat for 1 hour, stirring occasionally. Remove and discard the ham hock. Cook for 3 hours or until the beans are tender, stirring occasionally and adding more water to the saucepan if necessary. (Be careful not to burn the beans.) Crush ¹/3 to ¹/2 of the beans against the side of the pan to thicken the soup. Remove and discard the bay leaves before serving.

Yield: 6 to 8 servings

Italian Onion Soup

4 slices pancetta or bacon
¹/4 cup olive oil
6 large white onions, very
  thinly sliced
6 cups chicken stock
32 ounces diced tomatoes
1¹/2 teaspoons basil
¹/4 teaspoon freshly ground pepper
3 eggs, beaten
3 tablespoons grated
  Parmesan cheese

Sauté the pancetta in the olive oil in a stockpot over medium heat until the pancetta begins to brown. Add the onions and sauté until the onions are tender and translucent. Stir in the chicken stock, undrained tomatoes, basil and pepper. Bring to a boil. Reduce the heat. Simmer for at least 1 hour. Stir in the eggs and cheese just before serving. Cook until heated through; do not boil or the eggs will curdle.

Note: Use homegrown tomatoes and fresh basil, if possible. If using fresh basil, use 1 tablespoon chopped.

Yield: 4 to 6 servings

Butternut Lobster Bisque

LOBSTER STOCK

Crack four lobster shells into small pieces. Place the lobster heads and shells in a pot and cover with cold water. Bring to a boil. Reduce the heat and simmer for 15 minutes; strain.

3 tablespoons unsalted butter

2 cups chopped yellow onions

1 bay leaf

4 cups diced butternut squash (¹/₂-inch cubes)

1 tablespoon butter

1 cup chopped fresh lobster meat

2¹/₄ teaspoons fine sea salt

¹/₈ teaspoon white pepper

¹/₈ teaspoon cayenne pepper

1 bouquet garni (basil, thyme, garlic)

¹/₂ cup lobster stock

6 cups heavy cream or milk

1 tablespoon butter

¹/₂ teaspoon finely chopped fresh sweet basil for garnish

Melt 3 tablespoons butter in a 4-quart saucepan over medium-high heat. Add the onions and bay leaf. Cook for 4 to 5 minutes or just until the onions begin to brown, stirring constantly. Reduce the heat to medium. Add the butternut squash. Cook for 7 to 8 minutes or until the squash begins to soften and turn brown, stirring occasionally. Reduce the heat to low. Add 1 tablespoon butter and the lobster. Cook for 15 minutes, stirring occasionally. Add the salt, white pepper, cayenne pepper and bouquet garni. Cook for 3 to 4 minutes, stirring constantly and scraping the bottom and side of the saucepan with a wooden spoon. Add the lobster stock. Simmer for 3 to 4 minutes. Remove and discard the bay leaf and bouquet garni.

Process the lobster mixture in batches in a food processor until smooth. Return to the saucepan. Add the cream. Bring to a boil. Reduce the heat to low. Simmer for about 5 minutes. Stir in 1 tablespoon butter just before serving. Garnish with the basil.

Yield: 8 servings

Mario's Seafood Soup

2 teaspoons olive oil
2 red onions, sliced
2 garlic cloves, crushed
2 tablespoons red wine vinegar
12 cups fresh fish stock
2 (14-ounce) cans diced tomatoes
1 1/4 cups dry red wine
1 tablespoon chopped
    fresh rosemary
1 1/4 pounds halibut fillets, skinned
    and cut into 1-inch pieces
1 3/4 pounds mussels, scrubbed
8 ounces baby squid, cleaned,
    trimmed and sliced into rings
8 ounces fresh tiger shrimp, peeled
    and deveined
Salt and pepper to taste
6 to 8 slices French bread, toasted
    and rubbed with a cut
    garlic clove
Lemon wedges

Heat the olive oil in a large nonstick saucepan. Add the onions and garlic. Cook for 3 minutes, stirring constantly. Stir in the vinegar. Cook for 2 minutes. Stir in the fish stock, undrained tomatoes, wine and rosemary. Bring to a boil. Reduce the heat. Simmer for 10 minutes.

Stir in the halibut, mussels and squid and mix well. Simmer, covered, for 5 minutes or until the halibut is opaque. Stir in the shrimp. Simmer, covered, for 2 to 3 minutes or until the shrimp turn pink and the mussels open. (Discard any mussels that remain closed.) Season with salt and pepper.

Place a slice of garlic bread in the bottom of each of 6 to 8 warmed soup bowls. Ladle the soup over the bread. Serve with lemon wedges.

Yield: 6 to 8 servings

It is best to serve wine that has not been chilled for more than two weeks. Do not let it return to room temperature once it has been chilled. For white and rosé wines, chill for one to two hours. For Champagnes, chill for three to six hours. Red wines are served at a cool room temperature, around 60 degrees. Dessert wines can be served either chilled or at cool room temperature.

Let's Do Brunch

chapter three

Decadent French Toast

Stuffed French Toast with

Orange Marmalade Sauce

Sunday Scones

Old South Hot Water Corn Cakes

Buttermilk Pancakes

Perfect Blueberry Muffins

Six-Week Bran Muffins

Peach Muffins from

The Chickadee Cottage Cookbooks

Strawberry Muffins

Yeast Rolls

Angel Biscuits

Popovers

Best Banana Bread

Pineapple Banana Bread

Cranberry Orange Bread with

Streusel Topping

Old-Fashioned Gingerbread

Poppy Seed Bread

Chocolate Chip Pumpkin Bread

Pumpkin Bread

Strawberry Bread

Golden Grits Casserole

Egg Soufflé

Fiesta Quiche

Piecrust

Chicken Spectacular

Anna's Baked Fruit

Wheezie's Tea Cakes

Decadent French Toast

MIMOSA

Combine 2 1/2 ounces chilled Champagne and 2 1/2 ounces cold freshly squeezed orange juice in a Champagne glass and mix gently. This goes well with a brunch menu.

4 eggs
1/3 cup milk
1 teaspoon vanilla extract, or
    1 1/2 teaspoons imitation vanilla
1/8 teaspoon nutmeg
1 tablespoon butter
9 slices Texas toast or thick-cut
    French bread
1 cup sliced strawberries
1/4 cup confectioners' sugar
Pure maple syrup, warmed

Beat the eggs, milk, vanilla and nutmeg in a shallow dish; set aside.

Heat a griddle over medium-high heat. Add the butter; cook until melted. Dip the bread slices 1 at a time into the egg mixture, turning to soak both sides. Cook on the hot, buttered griddle until lightly browned on both sides.

Remove to a warm plate. Top with the strawberries and sprinkle with the confectioners' sugar. Serve with maple syrup.

Note: You may add 1/2 teaspoon banana extract to the egg mixture and top with sliced bananas. This is a great recipe to serve on New Year's Day with mimosas.

Yield: 9 servings

Stuffed French Toast with Orange Marmalade Sauce

8 ounces cream cheese, softened

$1/2$ cup part-skim ricotta cheese

$1/4$ cup orange marmalade

2 tablespoons sugar

1 (16-ounce) loaf sliced Vienna or
    Italian bread

4 eggs

1 cup milk

1 teaspoon vanilla extract

Nutmeg to taste

Orange Marmalade Sauce (below)

Preheat the oven to 475 degrees. Beat the cream cheese in a bowl until smooth. Beat in the ricotta cheese, orange marmalade and sugar. Discard the ends of the bread. Spread about 3 tablespoonfuls of the cream cheese mixture over 1 bread slice. Top with 1 bread slice, forming a sandwich. Repeat the procedure using the remaining bread slices and the remaining cream cheese mixture.

Beat the eggs in a shallow dish. Add the milk and vanilla and mix well. Dip the sandwiches 1 at a time into the egg mixture, turning to soak both sides. Place in a single layer on a greased baking sheet. Sprinkle with nutmeg. Bake for 5 minutes or until golden brown. Turn over and sprinkle with nutmeg. Bake for 3 to 5 minutes or until golden brown and slightly crisp. Serve immediately with Orange Marmalade Sauce.

Yield: 6 servings

Orange Marmalade Sauce

16 ounces orange marmalade

$3/4$ cup maple syrup

6 tablespoons butter

$1/2$ teaspoon nutmeg

Combine the orange marmalade, maple syrup, butter and nutmeg in a saucepan and mix well. Bring to a simmer, stirring constantly. Serve.

Note: You may stir chopped fresh peaches into the sauce.

1978 - *Friends of the Children's Hospital underwrites two wheelchairs for the neurosurgery department.*

Sunday Scones

2 cups unbleached flour

1 tablespoon baking powder

1 teaspoon sugar

1/2 teaspoon salt

5 tablespoons unsalted butter,
   cut into pieces

3/4 cup half-and-half

Photo on page 68.

Preheat the oven to 450 degrees. Combine the flour, baking powder, sugar and salt in a bowl and mix well. Cut in the butter until crumbly. Stir in the half-and-half until the dry ingredients are moistened. Shape the dough into a ball. Knead the dough on a lightly floured surface for 30 seconds. Roll into a 3/4-inch-thick circle. Place on a baking sheet. Cut into 8 wedges. Bake for 14 minutes.

Yield: 8 scones

Old South Hot Water Corn Cakes

1 cup quick-cooking grits

1/2 cup flour

1 egg, lightly beaten

1 tablespoon butter

1 teaspoon sugar

1/2 teaspoon salt

2 cups hot water

2 tablespoons shortening

Combine the grits, flour, egg, butter, sugar and salt in a heavy saucepan and mix well. Add the hot water gradually, stirring constantly. Bring to a boil. Reduce the heat to low. Cook for 2 minutes, stirring constantly. Remove from the heat. Let stand, covered, for 15 to 20 minutes or until cool enough to handle.

Shape 2 tablespoonfuls of the batter at a time into a ball and gently flatten into a 1/3-inch-thick circle. Heat the shortening in a heavy skillet over medium-high heat. Add the corn cakes. Cook for 5 minutes per side or until lightly browned. Drain on paper towels. Serve hot.

Note: These corn cakes pair well with a variety of soups and salads. Corn cakes may be made up to a day ahead. Cover the uncooked corn cakes with plastic wrap and refrigerate until ready to cook.

Yield: 6 servings

Buttermilk Pancakes

2 cups flour
1/4 cup granulated sugar
2 tablespoons brown sugar
1 tablespoon baking powder
1 teaspoon baking soda
1/2 teaspoon salt
2 cups buttermilk
3 egg yolks
6 tablespoons unsalted butter,
    melted
1 tablespoon vanilla extract
3 egg whites
6 tablespoons (about) unsalted
    butter, melted
1 cup strawberries, sliced
1 cup blueberries
2 bananas, sliced

Combine the flour, granulated sugar, brown sugar, baking powder, baking soda and salt in a large bowl; set aside. Whisk the buttermilk, egg yolks, 6 tablespoons butter and vanilla in a bowl; set aside. Beat the egg whites in a mixing bowl until soft peaks form; set aside.

Heat a skillet or griddle over medium-high heat until a drop of batter sizzles. Brush 1 tablespoon butter evenly over the surface.

Add the dry ingredients to the buttermilk mixture and stir just until mixed. Gently fold in the egg whites just until blended; do not overmix.

Pour a small amount of the batter at a time into the hot skillet. Cook for 2 to 3 minutes or until bubbles appear on the surface and the underside is golden brown. Turn the pancake. Cook until golden brown. Brush the skillet with the remaining butter as needed during cooking. Serve immediately topped with strawberries, blueberries and bananas.

Note: For blueberry pancakes, fold 1 to 2 cups blueberries into the batter before cooking.

Photo on page 65.

Yield: 8 servings

1980 - *The Children's Hospital staff expands to include 44 board-certified physicians.*

Perfect Blueberry Muffins

1 3/4 cups flour
2 teaspoons baking powder
1/4 teaspoon salt
1 cup fresh or frozen blueberries
3/4 cup milk
1/2 cup sugar
1/4 cup vegetable oil
1 teaspoon vanilla extract
2 egg whites, at room temperature

Preheat the oven to 350 degrees. Combine the flour, baking powder and salt in a large bowl and mix well. Add the blueberries and toss to coat, keeping the blueberries intact. Make a well in the center. Mix the milk, sugar, oil and vanilla in a bowl. Pour into the well and stir until the dry ingredients are moistened. Beat the egg whites in a mixing bowl until soft peaks form. Fold into the batter. Fill greased muffin cups 2/3 full. Bake for 20 minutes or until the muffins test done. Remove to a wire rack to cool.

Yield: 1 dozen muffins

We all have trouble getting muffins from the pan. Here's a tip that will have your muffins poppin' fresh out of the tin. Spray the tins with cooking spray before you load them just for added insurance. Place a wet towel beneath the hot pan, and they'll lift out easily and perfectly every time.

Six-Week Bran Muffins

1 (15-ounce) package bran flakes
   with raisins
5 cups flour
3 cups sugar
5 teaspoons baking soda
1 teaspoon salt
1 quart buttermilk
1 cup shortening, melted, or
   1 cup vegetable oil
4 eggs, beaten

Combine the cereal, flour, sugar, baking soda and salt in a large bowl and mix well. Stir in the buttermilk, shortening and eggs. Refrigerate in a covered container for up to 6 weeks. Preheat the oven to 400 degrees. Fill greased muffin cups 2/3 full. Bake for 15 to 20 minutes or until the muffins test done. Remove to a wire rack to cool.

Yield: 5 dozen muffins

Peach Muffins from The Chickadee Cottage Cookbooks

Instead of letting those mismatched cups and saucers sit in the cabinet, pull them out and use them at your next brunch or ladies' luncheon. Place chicken, egg, or tuna salad in a teacup and place on a plate or a saucer. Put a small Angel Biscuit or mini-muffin on the saucer's edge and put it on a clear glass plate. Simply hand the plate to each guest. This is a wonderful way to use your grandmother's china without worrying that everything doesn't match!

1¹/2 cups flour

1 cup sugar

³/4 teaspoon salt

¹/2 teaspoon baking soda

2 eggs

¹/2 cup vegetable oil

¹/2 teaspoon vanilla extract

¹/4 teaspoon almond extract

1¹/4 cups coarsely chopped
   peeled peaches

¹/2 cup chopped toasted almonds

Preheat the oven to 375 degrees. Combine the flour, sugar, salt and baking soda in a large bowl. Beat the eggs, oil, vanilla and almond extract in a mixing bowl. Add to the dry ingredients and stir just until moistened. Fold in the peaches and almonds.

Fill greased muffin cups ³/4 full. Bake for 20 minutes or until the muffins test done. Remove to a wire rack to cool.

Note: You may substitute one 16-ounce can drained and chopped peaches for the fresh peaches. Thank you to The Chickadee Cottage for sharing this delectable recipe with us.

Yield: 1 dozen muffins

1980 - *The new Children's Hospital is officially dedicated on September 15.*

Strawberry Muffins

2 cups flour
2/3 cup sugar
1 1/2 tablespoons baking powder
3/4 teaspoon salt
1 (10-ounce) package frozen sliced
    strawberries, thawed
2/3 cup milk
2 eggs
1/3 cup vegetable oil
Strawberry Butter (below)

Preheat the oven to 375 degrees. Combine the flour, sugar, baking powder and salt in a large bowl. Make a well in the center. Reserve 2 tablespoons of the undrained strawberries for the Strawberry Butter. Combine the remaining undrained strawberries, milk, eggs and oil in a bowl and mix well. Pour into the well and stir just until the dry ingredients are moistened.

Fill greased muffin cups 2/3 full. Bake for 20 minutes or until the muffins test done. Remove from the muffin cups immediately. Serve with Strawberry Butter.

Yield: 14 muffins

Strawberry Butter

1/2 cup (1 stick) butter, softened
2 tablespoons reserved strawberries

Combine the butter and strawberries in a bowl and mix well.

Yeast Rolls

1 envelope dry yeast
1/4 cup lukewarm (110-degree) water
2 eggs
1/2 cup sugar
1 teaspoon salt
2 cups flour
1 1/4 cups water
1/2 cup vegetable oil
3 cups flour
1/4 cup (1/2 stick) butter, melted

Dissolve the yeast in the lukewarm water in a bowl. Add the eggs, sugar and salt and mix well. Stir in 2 cups flour. Add the water and oil alternately with 3 cups flour, mixing well after each addition.

Roll the dough out on a lightly floured surface. Cut with a 2-inch biscuit cutter. Dip each circle halfway into the melted butter, then fold in half. Place in greased 9×13-inch baking pans. Let rise in a warm place for 2 to 3 hours or until doubled in bulk. Preheat the oven to 400 degrees. Bake the rolls for 15 minutes.

Yield: 3 dozen rolls

Angel Biscuits

2 cups unbleached flour
3 1/2 teaspoons sugar
1 teaspoon baking powder
1/2 teaspoon baking soda
1/2 teaspoon salt
3 1/2 tablespoons shortening
1 envelope dry yeast
1/4 cup lukewarm (110-degree) water
1/2 cup buttermilk

Combine the flour, sugar, baking powder, baking soda and salt in a bowl and mix well. Cut in the shortening until crumbly. Dissolve the yeast in the warm water. Add the yeast mixture and buttermilk to the dry ingredients and mix well.

Roll the dough 1/4 inch thick on a lightly floured surface. Cut with a floured biscuit cutter. Place on a well-greased baking sheet. Let rise, covered with waxed paper, in a warm place for 30 minutes. Preheat the oven to 425 degrees. Uncover the biscuits. Bake for 10 minutes.

Yield: 12 to 14 biscuits

Popovers

1¹/2 cups flour, sifted

1¹/2 cups milk

3 eggs

³/4 teaspoon kosher salt

1¹/2 tablespoons unsalted
   butter, melted

Preheat the oven to 425 degrees. Butter 12 popover cups or custard cups. Preheat the cups in the oven for 2 minutes before filling with the batter.

Whisk the flour, milk, eggs, salt and butter in a bowl until smooth; batter will be thin. Fill the hot popover cups 1/2 full. Bake for 30 minutes; do not overbake. Serve hot.

Yield: 1 dozen popovers

Best Banana Bread

3 medium or 4 small ripe
    bananas, mashed
1¹/2 cups flour
1 cup sugar
1 cup chopped pecans (optional)
¹/4 cup (¹/2 stick) butter or
    margarine, melted
1 egg
1 teaspoon baking soda
1 teaspoon salt

Preheat the oven to 325 degrees. Combine the bananas, flour, sugar, pecans, butter, egg, baking soda and salt in a bowl and mix well. Pour into a greased and floured loaf pan.

Bake for 1 hour or until lightly browned and a wooden pick inserted into the center comes out clean. Slice and serve warm with butter.

Note: This recipe may be doubled. Freeze the extra loaf to serve later. The riper the bananas, the sweeter and better this bread will taste.

Yield: 1 loaf

Pineapple Banana Bread

3 cups flour
2 cups sugar
1 teaspoon baking soda
1 teaspoon salt
2 cups mashed extra-ripe bananas
1 cup canola oil
1 (8-ounce) can crushed pineapple
1¹/2 teaspoons vanilla extract
¹/4 cup chopped pecans (optional)

Preheat the oven to 350 degrees. Combine the flour, sugar, baking soda and salt in a bowl and mix well. Add the bananas, canola oil, undrained pineapple and vanilla and mix well. Stir in the pecans. Pour into 2 greased loaf pans. Bake for 1 hour or until the loaves test done. Remove to a wire rack to cool.

Note: This is a very moist banana bread.

Yield: 2 loaves

Photo on page 79.

Cranberry Orange Bread with Streusel Topping

STREUSEL TOPPING

1/2 cup packed brown sugar

1/2 cup chopped walnuts

1/4 cup flour

1/2 teaspoon ground cinnamon

1/4 teaspoon salt

*3 tablespoons cold unsalted butter,
    cut into pieces*

BREAD

2 cups flour

3/4 cup sugar

1 1/2 teaspoons baking powder

1/2 teaspoon baking soda

1/2 teaspoon ground cinnamon

1/4 cup (1/2 stick) butter, softened

3/4 cup orange juice

1 egg

1 teaspoon grated orange zest

1 cup cranberries

1/2 cup chopped walnuts

Photo on page 79.

Preheat the oven to 350 degrees.
Grease the bottom only of a loaf pan.

For the streusel topping, combine the
brown sugar, walnuts, flour, cinnamon
and salt in a bowl. Cut in the butter
until crumbly; set aside.

For the bread, combine the flour,
sugar, baking powder, baking soda and
cinnamon in a bowl and mix well. Stir
in the butter until crumbly. Add the
orange juice, egg and orange zest and
stir just until moistened. Stir in the
cranberries and walnuts. Pour into the
prepared pan. Sprinkle with the
streusel topping.

Bake for 55 to 60 minutes or until the
topping is browned and a wooden pick
inserted into the center comes out clean.
Cool in the pan for 5 minutes. Remove
to a wire rack to cool completely.

Note: For muffins, fill greased muffin
cups 2/3 full. Bake for 10 to 12 minutes
or until a wooden pick inserted into
the center comes out clean.

Yield: 1 loaf

*Too brown too fast? If your baked
goods get brown before the inside is
cooked, try adding a heatproof dish
of water to the oven. The added
moisture will slow the browning
process and keep your baked goods
moist and perfect.*

1982 - *The Children's Hospital collaborates with 22 other hospitals as a founding member of the
Children's Miracle Network.*

 77

Old-Fashioned Gingerbread

1/3 cup butter or margarine,
     softened
1/2 cup sugar
1 cup molasses
1 egg or equivalent egg substitute
2 1/2 cups flour
1 1/2 teaspoons baking soda
1 teaspoon ground ginger
1 teaspoon ground cinnamon
1/2 teaspoon salt
1/2 teaspoon ground cloves
1 cup hot water
Warm Lemon Glaze (below)

Photo on page 79.

Preheat the oven to 350 degrees. Beat the butter in a mixing bowl at medium speed until light and fluffy. Add the sugar gradually, beating constantly. Add the molasses and egg and beat well. Combine the flour, baking soda, ginger, cinnamon, salt and cloves. Add to the creamed mixture alternately with the hot water, mixing well after each addition. Pour into a 9×9-baking pan coated with nonstick cooking spray.

Bake for 40 minutes or until a wooden pick inserted into the center comes out clean. Cool in the pan for 10 minutes. Pour the Warm Lemon Glaze over the top. Cut into squares and serve immediately.

Yield: 8 servings

Warm Lemon Glaze

1 cup sifted confectioners' sugar
1 1/2 tablespoons fresh lemon juice
1 1/2 teaspoons water
1/2 teaspoon vanilla extract
1/4 teaspoon grated lemon zest

Combine the confectioners' sugar, lemon juice, water, vanilla and lemon zest in a saucepan. Cook over low heat until warm, stirring frequently.

1983 - *The Neonatal Intensive Care Unit's Bereavement Program is established to help parents cope with the death of an infant.*

Poppy Seed Bread

A monthly breakfast is prepared by Friends of Williamson County and served to the patients and their families. This assortment of breads is an example of some of those homemade goodies.

BREAD

3 cups flour

2 cups sugar

1¹/₂ cups vegetable oil

1¹/₂ cups milk

3 eggs

2 tablespoons poppy seeds

2 teaspoons vanilla extract

2 teaspoons butter flavoring

1¹/₂ teaspoons baking powder

1¹/₂ teaspoons salt

GLAZE

³/₄ cup sugar

¹/₄ cup orange juice

¹/₂ teaspoon vanilla extract

¹/₂ teaspoon butter flavoring

Photo on page 79.

For the bread, preheat the oven to 325 degrees. Combine the flour, sugar, oil, milk, eggs, poppy seeds, vanilla, butter flavoring, baking powder and salt in a mixing bowl and beat for 2 minutes. Pour into 2 greased loaf pans.

Bake for 1 hour or until the loaves test done.

For the glaze, combine the sugar, orange juice, vanilla and butter flavoring in a bowl and mix well. Pour evenly over the hot loaves. Cool on a wire rack for 30 minutes. Remove from pans.

Note: Make up several of these bread recipes and bake them in tiny muffin tins so your guests can have a chance to taste all of them.

Yield: 2 loaves

1983 - *The Neil E. Green Fund is established to assist with buying wheelchairs, braces, and other equipment for children in the Junior League Home for Crippled Children.*

Chocolate Chip Pumpkin Bread

3 cups sugar

1 (15-ounce) can pumpkin

1 cup vegetable oil

4 eggs

2/3 cup water

3 1/2 cups flour

2 tablespoons baking soda

1 tablespoon ground cinnamon

1 tablespoon nutmeg

1 1/2 teaspoons salt

3/4 cup miniature semisweet
    chocolate chips

1/2 cup chopped walnuts

Preheat the oven to 350 degrees. Beat the sugar, pumpkin, oil, eggs and water in a mixing bowl until smooth. Blend in the flour, baking soda, cinnamon, nutmeg and salt. Fold in the chocolate chips and walnuts. Pour into 2 greased and floured loaf pans.

Bake for 1 hour or until a knife inserted into the center comes out clean. Cool in the pans for 10 minutes. Remove to a wire rack to cool completely.

Yield: 2 loaves

Photo on page 79.

Pumpkin Bread

3 cups sugar

1 cup vegetable oil

1 (15-ounce) can pumpkin

4 eggs, beaten

3 1/2 cups flour

2 teaspoons baking soda

2 teaspoons salt

1 teaspoon baking powder

1 teaspoon each ground nutmeg,
    cinnamon and allspice

1/2 teaspoon ground cloves

2/3 cup water

Preheat the oven to 350 degrees. Cream the sugar and oil in a mixing bowl. Add the pumpkin and eggs and mix well. Sift the flour, baking soda, salt, baking powder, nutmeg, cinnamon, allspice and cloves together. Add to the creamed mixture alternately with the water, mixing well after each addition. Pour into 2 well-greased and floured 5×9-inch loaf pans.

Bake for 60 to 70 minutes or until the loaves test done. Cool in the pans for 10 minutes. Remove to a wire rack to cool completely.

Yield: 2 loaves

Strawberry Bread

You'll be a hit at your next brunch or luncheon with this cute idea: In a small clay pot, plant any fresh herbs such as rosemary or lavender. With colorful ribbon, tie the guest's name on a note card, wrap it around the pot, and put it in front of each place. This makes a cute—and useful—party favor!

BREAD

3 cups flour

2 cups sugar

1 teaspoon baking soda

1 teaspoon salt

1 teaspoon ground cinnamon

2 (10-ounce) packages frozen strawberries, thawed

4 eggs, beaten

1 cup vegetable oil

ICING (OPTIONAL)

8 ounces cream cheese, softened

¹/4 cup reserved strawberry juice

Photo on page 79.

For the bread, preheat the oven to 350 degrees. Combine the flour, sugar, baking soda, salt and cinnamon in a large bowl and mix well. Make a well in the center. Reserve ¹/4 cup juice from the strawberries for the icing. Beat the strawberries, remaining juice, eggs and oil in a bowl. Pour into the well and stir with a wooden spoon just until the dry ingredients are moistened. Pour into 2 well-greased and floured 4×8-inch loaf pans.

Bake for 1 hour or until the loaves test done. Remove to a wire rack to cool.

For the icing, beat the cream cheese and strawberry juice in a bowl until smooth. Spread over the cooled loaves.

Note: This bread freezes very well.

Yield: 2 loaves

1984 - *Children's Hospital offers free group sessions for families with asthmatic children.*

Golden Grits Casserole

1 pound bulk pork sausage
3 cups hot cooked grits
2¹/2 cups (10 ounces) shredded
    sharp Cheddar cheese
1 tablespoon butter
1¹/2 cups milk
3 eggs, beaten

Preheat the oven to 350 degrees. Brown the sausage in a skillet, stirring until crumbly; drain. Remove to a 9×13-inch baking dish.

Combine the grits, cheese and butter in a bowl and mix well. Beat the milk and eggs in a bowl. Add to the grits mixture and mix well. Pour over the sausage. Bake for 1 hour.

Yield: 10 to 12 servings

Egg Soufflé

¹/2 cup (1 stick) butter, softened
6 ounces cream cheese, softened
2 pounds cottage cheese
6 eggs, beaten
1 cup flour
1 teaspoon baking powder
¹/2 cup sugar
2 teaspoons vanilla extract
¹/2 teaspoon ground cinnamon

Preheat the oven to 350 degrees. Cream the butter and cream cheese in a mixing bowl until light and fluffy. Add the cottage cheese, eggs, flour, baking powder, sugar and vanilla and mix well. Pour into a greased 9×13-inch baking pan. Sprinkle with the cinnamon.

Bake for 40 to 45 minutes or until lightly browned.

Yield: 8 servings

Fiesta Quiche

GRAPEFRUIT MARGARITAS

Moisten the rims of cocktail glasses with grapefruit quarters. Place salt on a saucer and swirl the rims of the glasses in the salt to coat the edges. Combine 6 ounces tequila, 3/4 cup grapefruit juice, 2 ounces triple sec, 2 tablespoons freshly squeezed lemon juice, 1/4 cup sugar, and 2 cups cracked ice in a blender container. Blend until smooth and pour into the prepared glasses. Place a grapefruit wedge on each rim. This makes 6 to 8 margaritas.

1 recipe Piecrust (page 86)
3 1/2 cups (14 ounces) shredded Monterey Jack cheese
3 1/2 cups (14 ounces) shredded sharp Cheddar cheese
2 medium tomatoes, seeded and sliced
1 (7-ounce) can diced green chiles, drained
1 (2-ounce) can sliced black olives, drained
2 tablespoons flour
6 egg yolks
1 (5-ounce) can evaporated milk
6 tablespoons flour
1/2 teaspoon salt
1/2 teaspoon oregano
1/4 teaspoon cumin
1/4 teaspoon pepper
6 egg whites
1/4 teaspoon cream of tartar
16 tomato slices for garnish

Photo on page 85.

Preheat the oven to 300 degrees. Roll the pastry on a lightly floured surface. Cut out and fit into 8 tartlet pans.

Combine the Monterey Jack cheese, Cheddar cheese, 2 sliced tomatoes, green chiles, olives and 2 tablespoons flour in a bowl and mix well. Divide evenly among the prepared tartlet pans.

Beat the egg yolks in a small bowl. Add the evaporated milk and 6 tablespoons flour alternately, beating until smooth. Stir in the salt, oregano, cumin and pepper; set aside.

Beat the egg whites with the cream of tartar in a mixing bowl until stiff, moist peaks form. Fold in the egg yolk mixture. Pour over the cheese mixture in the tartlet pans. Place 2 overlapping tomato slices on top of each quiche.

Bake for 40 minutes or until golden brown and firm to the touch. Let stand for about 15 minutes before serving.

Yield: 8 servings

1984 - The Junior League of Nashville helps to establish a Lung Center at Vanderbilt Children's Hospital, providing pulmonary care and treatment for children ages 1-14.

Piecrust

2 1/2 cups flour
2 tablespoons sugar
1 teaspoon salt
13 tablespoons unsalted butter,
    chilled and cut into
    1/2-inch cubes
1/2 cup shortening, chilled
4 to 6 tablespoons ice water

Process the flour, sugar and salt in a food processor until blended. Add the butter, pulsing 5 times. Add the shortening and pulse 4 or 5 times or until crumbly. Remove to a medium bowl. Sprinkle with 3 tablespoons of the ice water and mix well with a fork. Mix in enough of the remaining water 1 tablespoon at a time to make the dough hold together. Divide the dough into 2 balls, one slightly larger than the other. Flatten each into a 6-inch disk. Chill, wrapped in plastic wrap, for 30 minutes or longer.

Yield: 1 (2-crust) piecrust

Chicken Spectacular

1 (6-ounce) package long grain and
    wild rice mix
3 cups chopped cooked
    chicken breasts
2 cups French-style green beans,
    cooked and drained
1 (10-ounce) can low-fat, low-sodium
    cream of chicken soup
1 cup fat-free mayonnaise
1 onion, chopped
1/2 cup chopped celery
1 (8-ounce) can water chestnuts,
    drained and chopped
1 (4-ounce) jar sliced pimentos,
    drained

Preheat the oven to 350 degrees. Cook the rice mix according to the package directions, omitting the margarine. Combine the rice, chicken, green beans, soup, mayonnaise, onion, celery, water chestnuts and pimentos in a bowl and mix well. Spoon into a 2 1/2- to 3-quart baking dish. Bake for 25 to 30 minutes.

Yield: 16 servings

Photo on page 87.

1985 - Children's Hospital participates in a nationwide study of childhood brain tumors, pioneering a chemotherapy procedure administering eight drugs per child in one day.

87

Anna's Baked Fruit

For a festive touch at brunch or around the holidays, hollow a piece of citrus fruit, such as an orange, and put your favorite relish or cranberry sauce inside. The colors will be wonderful on your table.

2 cups chopped peeled Granny
    Smith apples (or any tart
    baking apples)
1 cup cranberries
1 cup sugar
3 tablespoons butter, melted
2 tablespoons unbleached flour
1 teaspoon ground cinnamon
1 cup granola
$1/2$ cup chopped pecans

Preheat the oven to 375 degrees. Toss the apples and cranberries with the sugar and butter in a bowl. Mix the flour and cinnamon in a small bowl. Sprinkle over the fruit mixture and toss to mix. Spoon into a 1-quart baking dish or 8 to 10 ramekins. Sprinkle with the granola and pecans.

Bake for 45 minutes or if using ramekins for 30 minutes, or until hot and bubbly.

May also be served warm with ice cream for dessert or as a side dish for chicken or pork.

Note: Place the ramekins on a baking sheet to catch any spills during baking.

Photo on page 87.

Yield: 8 to 10 servings

Wheezie's Tea Cakes

1 cup (2 sticks) butter, softened
1 cup granulated sugar
Grated zest of 2 lemons
3/4 cup half-and-half
3 eggs
2 tablespoons lemon juice
2 cups flour
1/4 cup poppy seeds
1 1/2 teaspoons baking powder
Pinch of salt
1 cup confectioners' sugar, sifted
2 to 3 teaspoons lemon juice
Sugared Pansies for garnish (below)

Preheat the oven to 350 degrees. Cream the butter and granulated sugar in a mixing bowl until light and fluffy. Reserve 2 teaspoons of the lemon zest. Add the remaining lemon zest, half-and-half, eggs and 2 tablespoons lemon juice to the creamed mixture and mix well. Stir in the flour, poppy seeds, baking powder and salt. Fill 24 greased muffin cups or medium fluted tartlet pans.

Bake for 14 to 18 minutes or until a wooden pick inserted into the center comes out clean. Remove to a wire rack.

Combine the confectioners' sugar and 2 to 3 teaspoons lemon juice in a bowl. Spread over the tea cakes while still warm. Garnish immediately with Sugared Pansies and the reserved lemon zest.

Yield: 2 dozen tea cakes

Sugared Pansies

24 small pesticide-free dried or
    fresh pansies
1 egg white
2 teaspoons water
1/4 cup superfine sugar
Edible glitter

Place the pansies on a waxed-paper-lined baking sheet. Beat the egg white and water in a small bowl. Brush the pansies gently with the egg white mixture using a clean small paintbrush. Sprinkle with the sugar and glitter. Let stand until completely dry. Remove from the waxed paper with a small spatula.

Note: If raw eggs are a problem in your area, use meringue powder and follow package instructions.

Dinner Is Served

chapter four

Beef Filets with Marsala

Beef Bourguignon

Beef Fondue from Chef Harry

Pepper Steak

Roasted Tenderloin of Beef in Black Pepper Sauce

Beef Wellington

Standing Rib Roast

Braised Short Ribs

Lasagna Bolognese

Ossobuco

Pineapple Baked Ham

Bow Tie alla Mario

Pork Tenderloin with Rosemary and Garlic

Marinated Pork Tenderloin with

Cranberry Orange Relish

Pork Tenderloin with Sun-Dried Tomatoes

Grilled Pork Chops

Grilled Marinated Lamb Chops

with Blackberry Jelly Sauce

Andouille Sausage and Black-Eyed Peas

Spice-Rubbed Hen with Roasted Root Vegetables

Chicken Marbella

Chicken Supreme

Chicken Scaloppini with Mushrooms

French Boneless Chicken

Grilled Chicken Stuffed with Basil and Tomato

Grilled Chicken with Black Bean Salsa

Pecan Chicken with Dijon Sauce

Chicken Didi

Parchment Baked Tilapia with Corn and Lime

Tommy's Grilled Salmon

New Potato-Crusted Red Snapper

Seared Ahi Tuna with Fried Green Tomatoes

Grilled Marinated Shrimp with Grit Cakes

Shrimp Scampi

Basantes' Fettucine Pancetta

President Reagan's Macaroni and Cheese

Lasagna Roll-Ups Florentine

Beef Filets with Marsala

LEMON SUGAR SNAP PEAS

Melt 2 tablespoons unsalted butter in a heavy skillet over medium heat. Add 2 pounds of fresh sugar snap peas and sauté for 3 minutes, stirring with a wooden spoon. Stir in 2 minced garlic cloves, 1 tablespoon freshly squeezed lemon juice, 2 teaspoons lemon zest, and salt and freshly ground black pepper to taste. Cook for 2 to 3 minutes or until hot. Garnish with red bell pepper strips.

1/4 cup olive oil
4 (3/4- to 1-inch) filets mignons
Freshly ground black pepper to taste
1/2 cup marsala
1/2 cup cabernet or other
*   good-quality red wine*
1 tablespoon tomato paste
1 1/2 teaspoons freshly minced garlic
1 teaspoon fennel seeds
1/4 to 1/2 teaspoon hot red
*   pepper flakes*
2 tablespoons chopped fresh parsley

Heat the olive oil in a large skillet until very hot. Add the filets. Cook over high heat for about 4 minutes per side, adjusting the heat as necessary to prevent the fat from burning. Remove to a plate; sprinkle with black pepper. Cover to keep warm.

Pour off all but 2 tablespoons of the drippings from the skillet. Add the marsala, cabernet and tomato paste. Cook over high heat, stirring and scraping up any browned bits. Boil for 30 seconds. Add the garlic, fennel seeds and red pepper. Reduce the heat to medium-high. Cook until the sauce is reduced to a syrupy consistency, stirring constantly.

Return the filets to the skillet, turning to cover both sides with the sauce. Remove to a serving plate and spoon the sauce over the top. Sprinkle with the parsley. Serve immediately.

Photo on page 93.

Yield: 4 servings

Physicians conduct a study of 51 infants diagnosed with neonatal necrotizing enterocolitis **1986 -** *during a five-year period. The study was published in the* American Journal of Diseases of Children.

Beef Bourguignon

3 pounds beef tenderloin

Salt and pepper to taste

2 to 3 tablespoons olive oil

4 slices bacon, chopped

2 garlic cloves, minced

2 cups dry red wine

2 cups beef stock

1 tablespoon tomato paste

1/2 teaspoon thyme

8 ounces pearl onions, peeled

1 (16-ounce) package
    baby-cut carrots

8 ounces mushrooms, sliced

1 1/2 tablespoons butter

1 tablespoon olive oil

2 tablespoons butter, softened

2 tablespoons flour

Cut the tenderloin into 1-inch-thick filets. Season both sides with salt and pepper. Heat 2 to 3 tablespoons olive oil in a large skillet. Add the filets and cook for about 3 to 4 minutes per side. (Do not overcook; beef should look a little red in the center.) Remove to a plate; set aside.

Cook the bacon in the drippings until browned and crisp. Remove to a plate; set aside.

Pour off all but 2 tablespoons of the drippings from the skillet. Add the garlic. Cook for about 2 minutes, stirring frequently. Add the wine. Cook over high heat, stirring to deglaze the skillet and scraping up any browned bits. Add the beef stock, tomato paste and thyme; season with salt and pepper. Bring to a boil. Reduce the heat and simmer for 15 minutes, stirring occasionally. Add the onions and carrots. Reduce the heat. Simmer for about 30 minutes or until the sauce is reduced and the vegetables are tender, stirring occasionally. Sauté the mushrooms in 1 1/2 tablespoons butter and 1 tablespoon olive oil in a separate skillet until tender.

If the sauce needs thickening, combine 2 tablespoons butter and flour in a bowl and mix well. Whisk into the sauce and cook until thickened, stirring frequently. Add the filets, bacon and mushrooms to the sauce. Simmer, covered, for 10 minutes.

Note: You may substitute drained jarred pearl onions for the fresh pearl onions.

Yield: 8 to 10 servings

Beef Fondue from Chef Harry

2 cups red wine

2 tablespoons freshly minced garlic

Fresh rosemary leaves to taste

1 pound lean steak, cut into
    1-inch cubes

1 pound lean pork loin, cut into
    3/4-inch cubes

1 quart peanut or vegetable oil

Sesame Scallion Dipping
    Sauce (below)

Wasabi Ginger Dipping
    Sauce (below)

Combine the wine, garlic and rosemary in a sealable plastic bag. Add the steak and pork; seal the bag. Marinate in the refrigerator for up to 2 hours. Drain, discardng the marinade. Pat the steak mixture with paper towels until completely dry. Heat the peanut oil to 370 degrees in a fondue pot according to the manufacturer's directions. Spear the steak and pork cubes on fondue forks. Deep-fry the steak to the desired degree of doneness and the pork until cooked through. To keep the oil at a consistent temperature, do not overcrowd the fondue pot. Drain on paper towels. Serve with Sesame Scallion Dipping Sauce and Wasabi Ginger Dipping Sauce.

Yield: 6 servings

Sesame Scallion Dipping Sauce

1 cup hoisin sauce

1 bunch scallions, chopped

2 tablespoons sesame seeds, toasted

1 garlic clove, minced

Combine the hoisin sauce, scallions, sesame seeds and garlic in a bowl and mix well.

Wasabi Ginger Dipping Sauce

1 cup mayonnaise

1 teaspoon ground ginger

Wasabi powder or paste to taste

Combine the mayonnaise, ginger and wasabi powder in a bowl and mix well.

Pepper Steak

You must never cook with any wine that you wouldn't drink so don't buy it in the first place!

2 pounds sirloin steak, cut into
   ¹/₈-inch strips
1 tablespoon paprika
2 garlic cloves, crushed
1 tablespoon butter or margarine
2 green bell peppers, cut into
   ¹/₂-inch strips
1 cup sliced green onions with tops
2 large tomatoes, diced
1 (10-ounce) can beef broth
¹/₄ cup plus 2 tablespoons water
3 tablespoons cornstarch
3 tablespoons soy sauce
3 cups hot cooked rice

Sprinkle the steak with the paprika. Let stand while assembling the remaining ingredients.

Cook the steak and garlic in the butter in a skillet until the beef is browned, stirring constantly. Add the bell peppers and green onions. Cook until the vegetables are wilted, stirring constantly. Stir in the tomatoes and beef broth. Bring to a boil. Reduce the heat. Simmer, covered, for 10 to 15 minutes. Blend the water, cornstarch and soy sauce in a bowl. Stir into the steak mixture. Cook until thickened, stirring frequently. Serve over the rice.

Yield: 6 to 8 servings

1987 - *The Sara Lee Classic golf tournament is initiated.*

Roasted Tenderloin of Beef in Black Pepper Sauce

Compliments of Sandy's Downtown Grill in Franklin

1 cup black peppercorns
1 (4¹/2-pound) beef
    tenderloin, trimmed
Salt to taste
2 tablespoons unsalted butter
¹/2 cup Cognac or other brandy
6 tablespoons unsalted butter

Preheat the oven to 500 degrees. Crush the peppercorns with a mortar and pestle or wrap in a clean kitchen towel and crush with a mallet. Season the tenderloin with salt and roll in the crushed pepper, coating all sides completely.

Melt 2 tablespoons butter in a large roasting pan. Add the tenderloin and sear quickly on all sides. Place the roasting pan in the oven.

Roast for 5 minutes; turn over the beef. Reduce the oven temperature to 400 degrees. Roast for 15 minutes for rare and 25 minutes for medium or until a meat thermometer registers 140 to 160 degrees. Remove the tenderloin to a platter, reserving the juices in the roasting pan; cover with foil. Let stand for 15 minutes.

Pour any accumulated drippings from the platter into the roasting pan. Add the Cognac. Cook over medium heat, stirring and scraping up any browned bits with a wooden spoon. Cut 6 tablespoons butter into small pieces. Whisk into the drippings until blended. Pour through a strainer into a sauceboat. Cut the beef into ¹/2-inch slices and arrange on a serving platter. Serve the sauce on the side or over the beef.

Yield: 8 servings

Beef Wellington

BEEF

1 (5-pound) beef tenderloin,
    well trimmed
1/4 cup (1/2 stick) unsalted butter,
    softened

DUXELLES (MUSHROOM STUFFING)

2 pounds mushrooms
1 cup chopped onion, or
    1/2 cup chopped shallots
1/2 cup (1 stick) butter
3/4 cup olive oil
1 teaspoon freshly grated nutmeg
Salt and freshly ground
    pepper to taste

ASSEMBLY

4 egg yolks
1/2 cup water
2 (17-ounce) packages frozen
    puff pastry (4 sheets),
    thawed
Salt and freshly ground
    pepper to taste
2 (4x2x2) cans pâté

For the beef, preheat the oven to 400 degrees. Rub the tenderloin with the butter. Place on a rack in a roasting pan. Roast for 25 minutes for very rare or until a meat thermometer registers 120 degrees.

For the duxelles, wrap the mushrooms in cheesecloth and squeeze over a bowl. Reserve the juice. Chop the mushrooms finely. Cook the onion in the butter and olive oil in a skillet until golden brown, stirring frequently. Stir in the mushrooms, reserved juice, nutmeg, salt and pepper.

To assemble, beat the egg yolks and water in a bowl. Unfold 1 sheet of puff pastry on a lightly floured surface. Roll into a square 6 inches wider than the beef and 6 inches deeper than needed to wrap around the tenderloin. Repeat with the remaining pastry sheets. Brush each pastry sheet lightly with the egg mixture, reserving a small amount. Overlap the pastry sheets to form 1 large square, sealing the seams. Pat the roasted tenderloin dry. Season with salt and pepper. Top with the duxelles and pâté. Center the tenderloin 4 inches from 1 edge of the pastry square and roll up to enclose in the pastry, folding in the ends. Moisten the edges of the pastry with some of the remaining egg mixture and press to seal completely. Place seam side down on a large baking sheet lined with foil or parchment paper. Cut vents in the top of the pastry to but not through the tenderloin. Brush the surface with the remaining egg mixture. Bake at 400 degrees for 10 minutes. Reduce the oven temperature to 350 degrees. Roast for 15 to 30 minutes or until the pastry is golden brown. Let stand for 15 minutes before slicing.

Photo on page 99.

Yield: 10 to 12 servings

Standing Rib Roast

2 garlic bulbs, roasted

1 teaspoon salt

1 tablespoon finely chopped
    fresh rosemary

1 tablespoon finely chopped
    fresh thyme

1/2 teaspoon freshly ground pepper

1 (6 1/2-pound) standing rib roast, fat
    trimmed in 1 strip and reserved

2 1/2 teaspoons salt

1 teaspoon freshly ground pepper

1 1/2 cups red wine

1/2 cup beef stock

Horseradish Cream Sauce (below)

Preheat the oven to 450 degrees. Separate the garlic bulbs into cloves. Squeeze the roasted garlic into a small bowl, discarding the garlic peel. Mash the garlic with a fork until almost smooth. Stir in 1 teaspoon salt, rosemary, thyme and 1/2 teaspoon pepper. Pat evenly over the surface of the roast. Place the reserved fat over the garlic mixture and tie in place with kitchen twine. Season the surface of the roast with 2 1/2 teaspoons salt and 1 teaspoon pepper.

Place the roast fat side up in a roasting pan. Pour the wine and beef stock into the pan. Roast for 20 minutes. Reduce the oven temperature to 350 degrees. Roast for 18 minutes per pound for rare and for 22 minutes per pound for medium or until a meat thermometer registers 140 to 160 degrees. Let stand for 20 minutes before carving. Remove the twine and discard the fat. Skim the fat from the pan drippings and serve alongside the roast. Serve with Horseradish Cream Sauce.

Yield: 8 servings

Horseradish Cream Sauce

1 cup whipping cream

1/2 cup horseradish, drained

1/2 cup mayonnaise

2 tablespoons Dijon mustard

Salt and pepper to taste

Beat the cream in a bowl until soft peaks form. Fold in the horseradish, mayonnaise, Dijon mustard, salt and pepper. Refrigerate, covered, until chilled.

1988 - Dr. Ian M. Burr becomes chairman of the Department of Pediatrics and medical director of the Children's Hospital.

Braised Short Ribs

3 pounds (3-inch) bone-in beef
    short ribs, well trimmed
1/2 teaspoon salt
1/4 teaspoon freshly ground pepper
1 tablespoon olive oil
2 onions, cut into halves and sliced
2 large carrots, chopped
1 tablespoon minced garlic
1/4 teaspoon salt
Rosemary Wine Sauce (below)

Preheat the oven to 350 degrees. Sprinkle the ribs with 1/2 teaspoon salt and pepper. Heat the olive oil in a Dutch oven over medium-high heat. Add the ribs. Cook until browned on all sides; remove to a plate and set aside.

Discard the drippings in the Dutch oven. Add the onions, carrots, garlic and 1/4 teaspoon salt. Cook over medium-low heat for 10 minutes or until the vegetables are tender. Return the ribs to the Dutch oven. Pour the Rosemary Wine Sauce over the ribs and vegetables. Bake, covered, for 2 hours or until the ribs are very tender and fall off the bones. Remove the ribs and vegetables to a serving platter; cover and keep warm. Skim the fat from the cooking liquid; discard the rosemary and any bones. Bring to a boil; pour over the ribs.

Yield: 6 servings

Rosemary Wine Sauce

1 carrot, chopped
1 yellow onion, chopped
4 large fresh rosemary sprigs
3/4 cup honey
1/2 cup raspberry vinegar
2 1/2 cups red wine (such as Merlot)
5 cups beef stock
Salt and pepper to taste

Combine the carrot, onion, rosemary and honey in a medium saucepan. Cook over medium-high heat until the vegetables are lightly browned and tender, stirring frequently. Add the vinegar and stir to deglaze the pan. Cook for 5 minutes, stirring occasionally. Reduce the heat to medium. Add the wine. Cook until the sauce is reduced to a syrupy consistency. Stir in the beef stock. Cook until the sauce is reduced to 3 cups. Season with salt and pepper.

Lasagna Bolognese

1 tablespoon extra-virgin olive oil

1 box or 8 to 10 fresh
     lasagna noodles

1 tablespoon extra-virgin olive oil

24 ounces small curd cottage cheese

15 ounces ricotta cheese

1 cup (4 ounces) freshly grated
     Parmesan cheese

1/4 cup half-and-half

1 egg

1 large garlic clove, minced

1 tablespoon dried chives

1 tablespoon freshly ground pepper

Bolognese Sauce (page 103)

4 cups (16 ounces) shredded
     mozzarella cheese

Italian seasoning to taste

Preheat the oven to 350 degrees. Grease a deep 9×13-inch baking pan with 1 tablespoon olive oil. Cook the lasagna noodles with 1 tablespoon olive oil according to the package directions. Drain on paper towels to remove any excess water; set aside.

Combine the cottage cheese, ricotta cheese, Parmesan cheese, half-and-half, egg, garlic, chives and pepper in a large bowl and mix well. Layer the noodles, cottage cheese mixture, Bolognese Sauce and mozzarella cheese 1/2 at a time in the prepared baking pan. Sprinkle Italian seasoning over the top. Place the pan on a baking sheet.

Bake for 30 to 45 minutes or until the center is bubbly. Let stand for 10 minutes before serving.

Note: You may divide the lasagna ingredients between two 9×9-inch baking pans. Bake and serve 1 immediately and take the other to a friend, or freeze to bake later.

Yield: 8 to 10 servings

Bolognese Sauce

1 to 1¹/₄ pounds ground sirloin
1 small onion, finely chopped
2 tablespoons beef bouillon
    granules
1 large garlic clove, minced
1 tablespoon oregano
1 tablespoon basil
¹/₂ teaspoon thyme
¹/₂ teaspoon sage
1 (15-ounce) can tomato sauce
1 (15-ounce) can petite
    diced tomatoes
1 (6-ounce) can tomato paste
¹/₄ to ¹/₂ cup dry red wine
¹/₄ cup milk

Brown the ground sirloin in a large saucepan, stirring until crumbly; rinse and drain. Add the onion, bouillon, garlic, oregano, basil, thyme and sage and mix well. Cook for 5 to 10 minutes or just until the onion is tender, stirring frequently. Add the tomato sauce, tomatoes, tomato paste, ¹/₄ cup wine and milk and mix well. Simmer for 30 to 35 minutes, stirring occasionally and adding enough of the remaining wine to reach the desired consistency if the sauce becomes too thick.

You may serve over pasta and garnish with freshly grated Parmesan cheese and chopped fresh basil.

Note: For a spicier sauce, substitute bulk pork sausage for half the ground sirloin. Recipe may be doubled or tripled.

Don't hesitate to use what you have around the house to make unusual table arrangements. Wine coolers can double as vases and add a festive touch to your party

Ossobuco

8 veal shank cross cuts,
    cut 1 1/2 inches thick
3/4 cup flour
3 tablespoons unsalted butter
3 tablespoons olive oil
1 yellow onion, minced
Salt and pepper to taste
1 1/2 cups dry white wine
2 1/2 cups meat stock
1/2 cup fresh flat-leaf parsley
1 small garlic clove
1 teaspoon grated lemon zest

Tie the veal shanks with kitchen twine. Coat with the flour. Heat the butter and olive oil in a large saucepan over medium heat. Add the veal shanks. Cook for 4 minutes or until golden brown. Turn over the shanks. Add the onion, salt and pepper. Cook for 4 minutes. Add the wine. Bring to a simmer. Cook for 1 minute. Add the meat stock. Bring to a simmer. Reduce the heat to low. Cook, covered, for 1 1/2 to 2 hours or until the veal is tender. Place the veal on a serving platter. Chop the parsley and garlic finely. Mix the parsley mixture and lemon zest in a bowl. Sprinkle over the veal. Pour the sauce over the top and serve.

Yield: 8 servings

Pineapple Baked Ham

1 fully cooked ham
1 tablespoon (or more) whole cloves
2 cups packed dark brown sugar
1 cup ginger ale
1 (8-ounce) can pineapple slices
Maraschino cherries for garnish

Preheat the oven to 350 degrees. Rinse the ham and pat dry. Score the surface fat in a diamond pattern, cutting about 1/4 inch deep. Stud with the cloves, inserting 1 into the center of each diamond. Pack the brown sugar loosely over the ham and cloves. Pour the ginger ale gently over the ham, being careful not to wash the brown sugar away. Arrange the pineapple slices on top of the ham. Place a maraschino cherry in the center of each slice, securing with wooden picks, if necessary.

Bake the ham according to package directions, allowing 15 to 20 minutes per pound, or until a meat thermometer registers 160 degrees and the glaze melts. Baste about every 20 minutes with the pan juices. Let stand before carving. Discard the cloves.

Yield: 4 ounces per serving

1989 - *The NICU initiates the Extracorporeal Membrane Oxygenation Program to provide prolonged heart-lung by-pass to infants, allowing their underdeveloped lungs to rest and heal.*

Bow Tie alla Mario

¹/4 cup (¹/2 stick) unsalted butter

1 tablespoon extra-virgin olive oil

2 ounces shredded prosciutto

1¹/2 cups mascarpone cheese

1¹/2 pounds bow tie pasta, cooked
   and drained

¹/2 cup fresh green peas or frozen
   green peas, thawed

Freshly ground pepper to taste

Heat the butter and olive oil in a heavy skillet over medium heat until the butter is melted. Add the prosciutto and toss to coat. Add the mascarpone cheese. Cook until melted, stirring constantly. Add the pasta and toss until well mixed. Add the peas and toss gently. Cook until heated through. Season with pepper and serve immediately.

Yield: 4 to 6 servings

Pork Tenderloin with Rosemary and Garlic

MARINADE FOR PORK TENDERLOIN OR SALMON

Process 1/2 cup vegetable oil, 3/4 cup soy sauce, 1/4 cup Worcestershire sauce, 2 tablespoons dry mustard, 11/2 teaspoons parsley, 1/2 teaspoon pepper, 1/2 cup wine vinegar, 1 chopped garlic clove, 1/3 cup lemon juice, a dash of oregano, and a dash of basil in a blender for 5 minutes. Pour over pork tenderloin or salmon in a sealable plastic bag. Marinate in the refrigerator. Drain, reserving the marinade. Baste the pork or salmon with the reserved marinade while cooking.

11/2 to 21/2 pounds pork
    tenderloin, trimmed
Softened butter
6 to 8 garlic cloves, thinly sliced
Fresh rosemary sprigs
Kosher salt and cracked pepper
Red wine

Photo on page 91.

Preheat the oven to 425 degrees. Rinse the pork; pat dry. Rub softened butter over the surface. Make several 1/2-inch-deep slits in the pork. Insert garlic slices and rosemary sprigs into each slit. Sprinkle with salt and pepper. Place the pork in a roasting pan and pour wine around the pork. Add any remaining garlic slices and rosemary sprigs to the pan.

Roast for 25 to 30 minutes or until a meat thermometer inserted into the thickest portion of the tenderloin registers 160 degrees, basting the pork with the pan drippings halfway through the roasting time. Cover the pan loosely with foil. Let stand for 5 to 8 minutes before slicing. Cut into 1/2-inch slices to serve.

Yield: 8 to 10 servings

  **1989** - *Phi Mu sponsors first 5K for Kids' Sake race.*

Marinated Pork Tenderloin with Cranberry Orange Relish

1 or 2 pork tenderloins (depending
    on size)
1 cup Cognac or other brandy
1 cup orange juice
1 tablespoon seasoned salt
1 teaspoon Cajun seasoning, or
    to taste
Cranberry Orange Relish (below)

Place the tenderloins in a sealable plastic bag. Pour the Cognac and orange juice over the pork; seal the bag. Marinate in the refrigerator for 4 to 12 hours.

Preheat the grill to 400 degrees. Remove the pork from the marinade, reserving the marinade. Sprinkle the pork with the seasoned salt and Cajun seasoning. Grill for 25 minutes or until a meat thermometer inserted into the thickest portion of the tenderloin registers 160 degrees, turning frequently and basting with the reserved marinade only during the first 10 minutes of the grilling time. Slice and serve with the warm Cranberry Orange Relish.

Yield: 8 to 10 servings

Cranberry Orange Relish

1 (12-ounce) package cranberries
1 large navel orange, peeled
    and chopped
1/2 cup fresh orange juice
1 tablespoon Cognac or
    other brandy
1 cup sugar
1 tablespoon cornstarch

Combine the cranberries, orange, orange juice and Cognac in a saucepan. Cook until the cranberries begin to pop and the mixture turns dark red, stirring constantly. Stir in the sugar and cornstarch. Cook to the consistency of gravy, stirring constantly and adding additional orange juice or Cognac if the relish becomes too thick.

Pork Tenderloin with Sun-Dried Tomatoes

1 large garlic bulb

2 tablespoons extra-virgin olive oil

1 teaspoon salt

1/2 teaspoon freshly ground pepper

4 (1-pound) pork tenderloins

1/2 cup dry red wine

1 tablespoon butter

12 sun-dried tomatoes,
  cut into strips

4 large mushrooms, sliced

1 1/2 cups dry red wine

2 fresh rosemary sprigs

1 3/4 cups beef broth

Preheat the oven to 400 degrees. Cut off and discard the top of the garlic bulb; wrap in foil. Bake for 30 minutes. Let stand until cool. Squeeze the garlic from the cloves.

Place 1 tablespoon of the garlic in a bowl, reserving the remaining garlic. Add the olive oil, salt and pepper and mix well. Rub over the surface of the tenderloins. Place the pork in a sealable plastic bag. Add 1/2 cup wine; seal the bag. Marinate in the refrigerator for 2 hours.

Melt the butter in a saucepan over medium heat. Add the sun-dried tomatoes and mushrooms. Sauté for 4 to 5 minutes. Add 1 1/2 cups wine and rosemary. Simmer for 20 minutes, stirring occasionally. Stir in the beef broth. Cook for 20 minutes longer. Remove and discard the rosemary sprigs. Stir in the reserved garlic. Cook for 2 minutes. Remove from the heat. Cover to keep warm and set aside.

Remove the tenderloin from the marinade, discarding the marinade. Grill the pork for 20 minutes or until a meat thermometer inserted into the thickest portion of the tenderloin registers 160 degrees, turning once. Let stand for 5 minutes. Cut into 1/2-inch slices; top with the sun-dried tomato mixture.

Yield: 8 to 10 servings

Grilled Pork Chops

6 bone-in pork chops

1 1/2 cups tamari

1 cup hoisin sauce

1 1/2 tablespoons sherry vinegar

1 1/2 tablespoons rice vinegar

1 tablespoon sugar

1 scallion with green top, minced

1 1/2 teaspoons grated fresh
     gingerroot

1 1/2 teaspoons minced garlic

1 teaspoon Tabasco sauce

1 teaspoon chili sauce

Freshly ground pepper to taste

1/4 cup fresh cilantro leaves
     for garnish

Place the pork chops in a sealable plastic bag. Combine the tamari, hoisin sauce, sherry vinegar, rice vinegar, sugar, scallion, gingerroot, garlic, Tabasco sauce, chili sauce and pepper in a bowl and mix well. Pour over the pork; seal the bag. Marinate in the refrigerator for 3 to 12 hours.

Remove the pork chops from the marinade, reserving the marinade. Grill the pork chops over hot coals for 5 to 10 minutes per side or until cooked through, basting with the reserved marinade. Garnish with the cilantro.

Yield: 6 servings

If you don't have time to cool your white or red wines before serving, add 2 or 3 frozen grapes to your glass. Use white grapes for white wine and red grapes for red wine. It will cool your wine, and you will have a snack at the bottom of the glass to boot!

Grilled Marinated Lamb Chops with Blackberry Jelly Sauce

1 cup frozen orange juice
    concentrate
1/2 cup water
1/4 cup soy sauce or tamari
Chopped fresh thyme, rosemary and
    oregano to taste
Salt and freshly ground pepper
    to taste
8 to 10 lamb chops
1/2 cup blackberry jelly
Juice of 1/2 orange
Couscous (page 111)
Blackberries for garnish

Combine the orange juice concentrate, water, soy sauce, thyme, rosemary, oregano, salt and pepper in a sealable plastic bag. Add the lamb chops; seal the bag. Marinate in the refrigerator for 30 to 60 minutes.

Remove the lamb chops from the marinade, reserving the marinade. Grill the lamb chops over hot coals for 10 minutes per side or until the juices run clear, basting with the reserved marinade only during the first 10 minutes of grilling.

Meanwhile, heat the blackberry jelly and orange juice in a small saucepan over low heat until the jelly is melted. Turn off the heat; cover and keep warm.

Drizzle the lamb chops with the blackberry jelly sauce. Serve with Couscous. Garnish each plate with a few blackberries.

Yield: 8 to 10 servings

Note: While lamb is traditionally served with mint jelly sauce, we wanted to use our favorite berry jelly to create a wonderful and unexpected taste. The orange juice cuts the sweetness of the jelly and complements the lamb.

1990 - The Junior League of Nashville donates 10 adapted toys designed for children who are quadriplegic, or have cerebral palsy, spina bifida, or spinal injuries.

Couscous

2 (10-ounce) packages
    plain couscous
1 cup toasted pine nuts
2 tablespoons chopped fresh chives

Prepare the couscous according to the package directions. Add the pine nuts and chives and toss to mix well.

Andouille Sausage and Black-Eyed Peas

1 1/2 pounds andouille
    sausage, sliced
1 pound frozen black-eyed peas
2 slices bacon, chopped
1 1/2 cups chopped onions
1 large green bell pepper, chopped
1 (16-ounce) can tomatoes,
    drained and chopped
1/4 cup chopped fresh parsley
2 tablespoons Allegro marinade or
    other soy-based meat marinade
2 garlic cloves, minced
1 teaspoon black pepper
1/2 teaspoon cayenne pepper
1/4 teaspoon oregano
1/4 teaspoon thyme
2 or 3 drops of Tabasco sauce
Salt to taste
Hot cooked rice

Sauté the sausage in a large skillet until cooked through; drain and set aside.

Cook the black-eyed peas in a small amount of water with the bacon, onions and bell pepper according to the package directions. Stir in the sausage, tomatoes, parsley, marinade, garlic, black pepper, cayenne pepper, oregano, thyme, Tabasco sauce and salt. Simmer for 30 minutes, stirring occasionally. Serve over rice.

Yield: 6 to 8 servings

1991 - *The Ann & Monroe Carell Jr. Family Chair in Pediatric Cardiology is funded.*

Spice-Rubbed Hen with Roasted Root Vegetables

1/4 cup olive oil

2 tablespoons grated fresh
     gingerroot

1 tablespoon grated lemon zest

1 tablespoon paprika

1 teaspoon salt

1/2 teaspoon freshly ground pepper

1 (41/2- to 5-pound) roasting hen

Roasted Root Vegetables (below)

Preheat the oven to 425 degrees. Whisk the olive oil, gingerroot, lemon zest, paprika, salt and pepper in a small bowl. Rinse the hen and pat dry. Rub 1/3 of the olive oil mixture over the inside of the hen cavity. Rub the remaining olive oil mixture over the outside surface of the hen. Place the hen in a roasting pan.

Roast for 11/4 hours or until the juices run clear and a meat thermometer inserted in the thickest part of the hen registers 180 degrees. Remove from the oven and place on a serving platter. Pour the pan drippings into a cup and skim off the fat. Drizzle the drippings over the hen just before serving. Serve with Roasted Root Vegetables.

Photo on page 113.

Yield: 4 servings

Roasted Root Vegetables

4 to 5 cups cut-up root or winter
     vegetables, peeled if desired
     (such as sweet potatoes, golden
     or purple beets, red or yellow
     onions, carrots, red potatoes or
     garlic bulbs)

2 to 3 tablespoons extra-virgin
     olive oil

Freshly ground pepper to taste

Kosher salt to taste

Preheat the oven to 375 degrees. If using garlic bulbs, cut off and discard the tops. Combine the olive oil, pepper and salt in a bowl. Add the vegetables and toss to coat. Place in a single layer in a heavy baking dish. Roast for 30 to 45 minutes or until tender, stirring occasionally and drizzling with additional olive oil.

Note: You may roast the vegetables with the chicken by adding them to the roasting pan 30 minutes before the chicken is done. Leaving the peeling on the vegetables helps the vegetables hold their shape and gives them better flavor.

1991 - Wal-Mart donates $117,000 to the Children's Miracle Network.

Chicken Marbella

1 cup pitted prunes

1/2 cup pitted Spanish green olives

1/2 cup capers, partially drained

1/2 cup red wine vinegar

1/2 cup olive oil

1/4 cup oregano

3 large garlic cloves, minced

4 bay leaves

Coarse salt and freshly ground
　　pepper to taste

10 to 12 boneless chicken breasts

1 cup packed brown sugar

1 cup white wine

1/4 cup fresh flat-leaf parsley or
　　cilantro, finely chopped

Combine the prunes, olives, capers, vinegar, olive oil, oregano, garlic, bay leaves, salt and pepper in a large bowl and mix well. Arrange the chicken in a large baking dish. Pour the prune mixture over the chicken. Marinate, covered, in the refrigerator for 4 to 12 hours.

Preheat the oven to 350 degrees. Sprinkle the brown sugar over the chicken. Pour the wine around the chicken. Bake for 50 to 60 minutes or until cooked through, basting frequently with the marinade. Remove and discard the bay leaves.

Remove the chicken, prunes, olives and capers with a slotted spoon to a serving platter. Top with a few spoonfuls of the marinade. Sprinkle with the parsley. Serve with the remaining marinade.

Note: You may substitute chicken quarters for the chicken breasts. May be cooled and served at room temperature.

Yield: 10 to 12 servings

Chicken Supreme

6 whole chicken breasts

1 cup sour cream

2 tablespoons fresh lemon juice

2 teaspoons salt

2 teaspoons Worcestershire sauce

2 garlic cloves, minced

1 cup bread crumbs

1/4 teaspoon paprika

1/4 teaspoon pepper

1 cup (2 sticks) butter, melted

Rinse the chicken and pat dry. Cut any large chicken breasts into single-serving pieces. Combine the sour cream, lemon juice, salt, Worcestershire sauce and garlic in a bowl and mix well. Coat the chicken with the sour cream mixture. Place in a bowl and top with the remaining sour cream mixture. Marinate, covered, in the refrigerator for 8 to 12 hours.

Preheat the oven to 350 degrees. Combine the bread crumbs, paprika and pepper in a bowl and mix well. Remove the chicken from the bowl, keeping as much of the sour cream mixture as possible on the chicken pieces. Coat with the bread crumb mixture. Place in a large baking dish. Pour 1/2 cup of the butter over the chicken.

Bake for 45 minutes. Pour the remaining 1/2 cup butter over the chicken. Bake for 15 minutes or until cooked through.

Yield: 6 to 8 servings

GINGERED CARROTS

Peel and cut 10 carrots into halves lengthwise and then into fourths. Boil in water to cover in a saucepan for 8 minutes or until tender-crisp. Drain and set aside. Melt 6 tablespoons butter in a skillet. Add 1/2 cup sugar and 1/2 teaspoon ground ginger. Reduce the heat and add the carrots. Cook until the carrots are glazed.

Chicken Scaloppini with Mushrooms

4 boneless skinless chicken breasts

$^1/_2$ cup flour

1$^1/_2$ teaspoons kosher salt

$^1/_2$ teaspoon freshly ground pepper

3 tablespoons vegetable oil

2 tablespoons unsalted butter

8 ounces mushrooms,
    finely chopped

$^1/_4$ cup dry white wine or marsala

1 cup chicken stock

2 tablespoons chopped fresh chives

2 tablespoons sour cream

Salt and freshly ground pepper
    to taste

Pound the chicken breasts $^1/_4$ inch thick between sheets of waxed paper; set aside.

Combine the flour, 1$^1/_2$ teaspoons salt and $^1/_2$ teaspoon pepper in a shallow dish. Heat 1$^1/_2$ tablespoons of the oil in a large skillet over medium-high heat. Coat the chicken with the flour mixture, shaking to remove any excess. Arrange in a single layer in the skillet. Cook for 4 minutes per side or until lightly browned and cooked through. Remove the chicken to a plate. Repeat until all of the chicken has been cooked.

Heat the butter in the skillet until melted. Add the mushrooms. Cook for about 5 minutes, stirring frequently. Stir in the wine. Increase the heat to high. Add the chicken stock and chicken. Simmer for 2 minutes or until the chicken is heated through and the sauce is thickened, turning the chicken frequently.

Remove the chicken to 4 individual serving plates. Stir the chives and sour cream into the sauce. Season with salt and pepper to taste. Spoon over the chicken.

Yield: 4 servings

1991 - The 17-bed Adolescent Unit is created in the round wing on the seventh floor of Medical Center North to treat sub-acute illness in children ages eight and older.

French Boneless Chicken

4 boneless skinless chicken pieces

Salt and freshly ground pepper
    to taste

Garlic powder to taste

3 tablespoons olive oil

2 tablespoons butter

1 onion, chopped

8 ounces mushrooms,
    cut into quarters

$1/3$ to $1/2$ cup white wine

1 cup (4 ounces) shredded
    mozzarella cheese

Preheat the oven to 350 degrees. Pound the chicken to a uniform thickness between sheets of waxed paper. Sprinkle with salt, pepper and garlic powder. Heat half the olive oil and half the butter in a skillet. Add the chicken. Sauté briefly; do not overcook. Remove to a baking dish.

Melt the remaining 1 tablespoon butter with the remaining $1^1/2$ tablespoons olive oil in the same skillet. Add the onion and sauté until tender. Add the mushrooms and sauté until tender. Stir in the wine. Simmer for a few minutes.

Sprinkle the cheese over the chicken. Top with the mushroom mixture. Bake for 30 to 45 minutes or until bubbly and the chicken is cooked through.

Yield: 4 to 6 servings

Grilled Chicken Stuffed with Basil and Tomato

To add flavor to grilled foods, sprinkle dried herbs such as oregano, rosemary, tarragon, or thyme over hot coals just before placing meats or vegetables on the grill. A wonderful aroma will permeate the air and the food. Fresh lemon halves squeezed over grilled meats just prior to serving enhances the flavor.

4 boneless skinless chicken breast halves (about 6 ounces each)
1/2 teaspoon coarse salt
Freshly ground pepper
2 garlic cloves, minced
1 tablespoon extra-virgin olive oil
12 fresh basil leaves
2 beefsteak tomatoes, cut into 1/4-inch slices
Fresh basil leaves for garnish

To butterfly the chicken breasts, place the chicken smooth sides down on a cutting board, placing the pointed ends toward you. Starting on 1 long side, split each chicken breast horizontally almost in half (stop cutting about 1/2 inch before reaching the opposite side). Open each cut chicken breast like a book. Sprinkle the surface of each with 1/8 teaspoon of the salt; season with pepper. Remove to a plate. Coat both sides with the garlic and olive oil. Let stand for 30 minutes.

Heat a grill or grill pan to medium. Place 3 basil leaves on 1 half of each opened chicken breast; top with 2 tomato slices. Close the chicken breasts and secure each with 2 wooden picks.

Grill the chicken for 15 minutes or until golden brown on both sides and cooked through, turning once. Remove to a serving platter; remove the wooden picks. Garnish with basil leaves.

Yield: 4 servings

Grilled Chicken with Black Bean Salsa

3 (16-ounce) cans black beans,
    rinsed and drained
1 (16-ounce) can whole kernel corn,
    rinsed and drained
1 (16-ounce) jar picante sauce
2 ribs celery, chopped
1 onion, chopped
1 green bell pepper, chopped
1 tomato, chopped
1 (4-ounce) can green chiles
1 red Fresno chile, minced
Chopped fresh cilantro to taste
1/4 cup olive oil
1/8 teaspoon chili powder
Pinch of cumin
1 tablespoon vinegar, or to taste
Hot red pepper sauce to taste
Salt and pepper to taste
6 boneless skinless chicken breasts
1 large red onion, thickly sliced
    into rings

Combine the black beans, corn, picante sauce, celery, chopped onion, bell pepper, tomato, green chiles, Fresno chile, cilantro, olive oil, chili powder, cumin, vinegar, pepper sauce, salt and pepper in a bowl and mix well. Refrigerate, covered, until chilled.

Preheat the grill. Grill the chicken and red onion until the chicken is cooked through and the onion is tender. Serve with the black bean salsa.

Yield: 6 servings

Pecan Chicken with Dijon Sauce

4 boneless chicken breast halves

1/2 cup (1 stick) butter, melted

3 tablespoons Dijon mustard

6 ounces pecans, finely chopped

1/4 cup (1/2 stick) butter

2 tablespoons canola oil or
   vegetable oil

2/3 cup sour cream

1 tablespoon Dijon mustard

1 teaspoon kosher salt

1/4 teaspoon freshly ground pepper

Preheat the oven to 350 degrees. Pound the chicken to a uniform thickness between sheets of waxed paper. Combine the melted butter and 3 tablespoons Dijon mustard in a shallow dish and mix well. Dip each chicken breast into the mustard mixture. Coat with the pecans; set aside.

Heat 1/4 cup butter and canola oil in a skillet. Add the chicken. Cook until lightly browned on each side. Remove to a baking pan. Bake for 30 minutes or until cooked through.

Drain the remaining butter and oil from the skillet. Heat the sour cream in the skillet, scraping up any browned bits. Stir in 1 tablespoon Dijon mustard, salt and pepper. Spoon the Dijon sauce onto serving plates; top with the chicken.

Yield: 4 servings

1992 - The Pediatric Intermediate Care Unit and the Pediatric Critical Care Unit open.

Chicken Didi

8 to 10 chicken breasts

4 ribs celery, cut into thirds

Salt to taste

1/2 cup (1 stick) butter

3 green bell peppers, cut into
   1/8-inch strips

1/2 cup flour

1 quart milk

1 teaspoon salt

Pepper to taste

Paprika to taste

1 pound mushrooms, sliced, or
   2 (6-ounce) cans sliced
   mushrooms, drained

1 (7-ounce) jar pimentos

2 cups heavy cream

1/2 cup dry sherry, or to taste

Hot biscuits, split, or toasted
   corn bread

Cook the chicken with the celery in a small amount of salted water in a saucepan until tender and cooked through. Let stand until cool. Reserve 1 cup of the chicken broth, discarding the celery. Cut the chicken into bite-size pieces, discarding the skin and bones; set aside.

Melt the butter in a heavy saucepan over low heat. Add the bell peppers. Sauté for about 5 minutes. Remove the bell peppers with a slotted spoon to a plate; cover. Add the flour gradually to the butter, stirring until blended. Add the milk and reserved chicken broth gradually, stirring constantly. Stir in 1 teaspoon salt, pepper and paprika. Cook over low heat until the sauce thickens, stirring constantly. Add the chicken, bell peppers, mushrooms and pimentos. Add the cream gradually, stirring constantly. Cook, covered, until the chicken is heated through. Stir in the sherry just before serving. Serve over biscuits.

Yield: 8 servings

TROPICAL MANGO SALSA

Peel and chop 2 ripe mangoes into small cubes and place in a nonreactive bowl. Squeeze the juice of 1 1/2 limes over the mangoes and toss gently to coat. Add 1/2 of a chopped bell pepper, 1/3 cup chopped purple onion, 1/2 of a chopped English cucumber, 1 minced small Fresno chile, and 1 tablespoon minced fresh cilantro and mix well. This will keep for several hours and goes well with grilled fish, seafood, or kabobs. You may substitute a pinch of red pepper flakes for the chile and mint for the cilantro.

1 (16-ounce) package frozen corn kernels, thawed and drained
1 red bell pepper, chopped
2 tablespoons chopped fresh cilantro
1/2 teaspoon chili powder
Salt and freshly ground pepper to taste
Olive oil
4 (8-ounce) skinless tilapia fillets
1 lime, cut into halves
Paper-thin lime slices
Tropical Mango Salsa (at left)

Preheat the oven to 450 degrees. Mix the corn, bell pepper, cilantro, chili powder, salt and pepper in a nonreactive mixing bowl.

Place a large sheet of parchment paper on a work surface. Fold the paper in half. Open the paper and spray the surface with nonstick cooking spray. Spoon 1/4 of the corn mixture onto 1 side of the parchment; drizzle with olive oil. Place 1 tilapia fillet on top. Squeeze some of the juice from the lime halves over the tilapia and vegetables. Season the tilapia with salt and pepper. Top with lime slices; drizzle with olive oil. Fold the other side of the parchment over the tilapia and vegetables. Seal by rolling up the edges to create a packet. Repeat the procedure using the remaining ingredients. Place the packets on a baking sheet.

Bake for 30 minutes or until the tilapia is opaque and flakes easily. Let stand for about 5 minutes. Remove each packet to a serving plate and cut open carefully with scissors. Serve with Tropical Mango Salsa.

Photo on page 123.

Yield: 4 servings

1992 - *Nurses in the Intermediate Care Nursery establish a program for community groups to sew clothing for infants.*

Tommy's Grilled Salmon

1 (1-pound) salmon fillet
3 tablespoons butter
2 tablespoons mayonnaise
1 lemon, cut into halves
1 tablespoon chopped
   fresh parsley
1 tablespoon chopped
   fresh dillweed
2 tablespoons drained capers

Let the salmon stand at room temperature for 30 minutes before grilling.

Preheat the grill to medium-high. Melt the butter in a small saucepan over low heat or in a small microwave-safe bowl in the microwave; set aside.

Brush the mayonnaise over both sides of the salmon. Squeeze the juice from 1 lemon half over both sides of the salmon. Grill skin side down for about 5 minutes. Turn over and cook for about 5 minutes or until the salmon is opaque and flakes easily. Remove to a serving plate.

Drizzle the melted butter over the salmon. Squeeze the juice from the remaining lemon half over the top and sprinkle with the parsley, dillweed and capers. Serve immediately.

Yield: 2 to 3 servings

Herb Butter

¹/₂ cup (1 stick) salted
   butter, softened
1 tablespoon lemon juice
1 tablespoon basil
1 teaspoon cilantro
1 teaspoon garlic salt

Place the butter in a deep bowl. Add the lemon juice, basil, cilantro and garlic salt. Mix with a fork until evenly blended; do not overmix. Spoon onto the center of a piece of plastic wrap. Shape into a log; wrap in the plastic wrap. Refrigerate for 1 day. Cut the herb butter into slices and place on top of hot cooked fish, meats and vegetables.

Yield: 8 to 10 servings

1992 - *The Junior League of Nashville Family Resource Center is created to provide easy access to health and medical information.*

New Potato-Crusted Red Snapper

1/2 cup prepared horseradish

1/2 cup sour cream

4 fresh red snapper fillets with skin

Salt and pepper to taste

12 ounces new potatoes, scrubbed

1/2 cup (1 stick) butter

Combine the horseradish and sour cream in a bowl and mix well. Refrigerate, covered, until chilled.

Preheat the oven to 450 degrees. Place the fillets skin side down on a baking sheet. Season with salt and pepper. Cut the potatoes into very thin slices using a mandoline or very sharp knife. (Slices should be as thin as potato chips.) Place the potato slices in a bowl of cold water as they are cut to prevent browning. Drain the potatoes and pat dry with paper towels. Arrange the potato slices on top of the fillets, beginning at the narrow end and moving toward the wide end, in a pattern that resembles fish scales. Place 2 tablespoons of the butter on each fillet.

Bake for 4 1/2 to 5 minutes or until the potatoes are light golden brown and the fillets flake easily. Serve with the horseradish mixture.

Note: You may substitute any flaky white fish for the red snapper.

Yield: 4 servings

1992 - The Junior League of Nashville funds the Chronic Disease Center. The program, which serves as a model for the nation, improves how doctors, staff, private and public agencies, and families work together in the ongoing treatment of chronically ill children.

Seared Ahi Tuna with Fried Green Tomatoes

Coarsely ground pepper

1 pound fresh ahi tuna

1/2 cup cornmeal

1 teaspoon mint

1 teaspoon ground cumin

1/2 teaspoon salt

1/2 cup buttermilk

3 large green tomatoes, cut
        into 1/4-inch thick slices

Vegetable oil for frying

1 tablespoon sesame oil

Mango Salsa (below)

Photo on page 127.

Pat the pepper onto both sides of the tuna; set aside.

Combine the cornmeal, mint, cumin, salt and buttermilk in a bowl and mix well. Dip the tomato slices into the batter, coating evenly. Fry in a skillet in 2-inch-deep hot oil over medium-high heat until golden brown.

Heat the sesame oil in a skillet over high heat. Add the tuna. Sear for 2 minutes or until the surface is white and the interior is pink.

To serve, place the fried green tomatoes on serving plates. Top with thin slices of tuna and Mango Salsa.

Yield: 4 to 6 servings

Mango Salsa

3 or 4 ripe mangoes, peeled
        and chopped

1/4 cup orange juice

1/4 cup chopped fresh cilantro

1 small red onion, chopped

1 teaspoon ground cinnamon

1 habanero chile,
        chopped (optional)

Combine the mangoes, orange juice, cilantro, onion, cinnamon and habanero chile in a glass bowl and mix well.

1992 - Children's Miracle Network Bowling for Miracles is initiated.

The National Institute of Diabetic, Digestive and Kidney Diseases awards a $2 million
1992 - grant to the Nephrology Center, one of two programs in the country funded and the only
one based in pediatrics.

127

Grilled Marinated Shrimp with Grit Cakes

24 large unpeeled shrimp

1/3 cup extra-virgin olive oil

1/4 cup fresh lime juice

2 tablespoons chopped
    fresh cilantro

2 tablespoons Worcestershire sauce

2 garlic cloves, crushed

1 teaspoon Tabasco sauce

Salt and pepper to taste

Grit Cakes (below)

Lime wedges for garnish

Split the shrimp shells up the back with a sharp knife to allow the marinade to penetrate the shells. Remove any large veins. Mix next 8 ingredients in a medium bowl. Add the shrimp and toss to coat. Marinate, covered, in the refrigerator for 2 to 3 hours.

Remove the shrimp from the marinade; discard the marinade. Preheat the grill. Grill over hot coals for 4 to 5 minutes or until the shrimp turn pink. Serve on a platter with Grit Cakes and lime wedges.

Note: The shrimp may be broiled for about 8 minutes rather than grilled.

Photo on page 127.

Yield: 12 servings

Grit Cakes

3 cups water

3/4 cup yellow grits

Freshly minced garlic or garlic
    powder (optional)

1 cup (4 ounces) shredded sharp
    Cheddar cheese

6 tablespoons butter

1 teaspoon salt

1 teaspoon paprika

Few drops of hot red pepper sauce

Olive oil for frying

Bring the water to a boil in a saucepan over medium heat. Add the grits gradually, stirring constantly. Stir in the garlic. Cook until the grits are thickened, stirring constantly. Remove from the heat. Add the cheese and butter and stir until melted. Stir in the salt, paprika and pepper sauce. Line a 12×17-inch baking pan with parchment paper or foil. Pour the grits into the pan. Chill for about 1 hour or until the grits are very firm.

Cut the chilled grits into squares of various sizes with a sharp knife. Heat olive oil in a heavy skillet over medium-high heat. Add the grit cakes and fry on both sides until crispy. Place on a baking sheet and keep warm in the oven until serving time.

Shrimp Scampi

4 garlic cloves, crushed
3 tablespoons olive oil
3 tablespoons butter
1¹/2 pounds peeled shrimp
1 cup dry white wine
¹/4 cup fresh lemon juice
¹/4 cup bread crumbs
¹/4 cup freshly grated
    Parmesan cheese
Salt and pepper to taste

Sauté the garlic in the olive oil and butter in an ovenproof skillet. Add the shrimp. Cook for 4 to 6 minutes or until the shrimp turn pink, turning frequently. Remove from the skillet; keep warm.

Add the wine to the drippings and stir to deglaze the skillet. Cook until reduced to ¹/3 cup. Add the lemon juice. Cook for 2 to 3 minutes, stirring occasionally. Return the shrimp to the skillet and toss to coat. Sprinkle the bread crumbs, cheese, salt and pepper over the shrimp. Broil for 1 minute. Serve immediately.

Yield: 4 servings

Basantes' Fettucine Pancetta

16 ounces uncooked fettucine
6 ounces pancetta, finely chopped
1 small yellow onion, finely chopped
³/4 cup chicken stock
1 teaspoon white pepper
¹/2 teaspoon nutmeg
2 cups heavy cream
2 cups (8 ounces) grated Parmesan
    and Romano cheese

Cook the fettucine according to the package directions; drain.

Cook the pancetta and onion in a skillet until caramelized, stirring frequently. Add the chicken stock and stir to deglaze the skillet. Stir in the pepper and nutmeg. Cook until the stock is almost completely reduced. Add the cream. Cook until the cream is reduced and thickened to the desired consistency. Add the pasta and cheese and toss to mix.

Yield: 4 servings

President Reagan's Macaroni and Cheese

Don't give your guests neck strain by putting table decorations at eye level. Flowers and candles should be either low enough for your guests to see each other or tall enough for the guests to see through.

8 ounces macaroni

1 egg, beaten

1 teaspoon margarine, melted

1 tablespoon hot water

1 teaspoon salt

1 teaspoon dry mustard

1 cup milk

3 cups (12 ounces) shredded sharp Cheddar cheese

2 cups (about) milk

1 cup (4 ounces) shredded sharp Cheddar cheese

Preheat the oven to 350 degrees. Cook the macaroni according to the package directions; drain. Place in a large bowl. Stir in the egg and margarine. Combine the water, salt and dry mustard in a bowl and mix well. Stir in 1 cup milk. Add the milk mixture and 3 cups cheese to the macaroni and toss gently but thoroughly. Spoon into a buttered 9×13-inch baking dish. Add enough of the 2 cups milk to cover. Sprinkle with 1 cup cheese. Bake for 45 minutes or until the custard is set and the top is crusty.

Note: This recipe is from 20 *Years of Good Taste*, Mission Viejo's 20th Anniversary Community Cookbook.

Yield: 6 servings

Lasagna Roll-Ups Florentine

2 (10-ounce) packages frozen
    spinach, thawed and
    well drained
1 cup ricotta cheese
1 cup (4 ounces) shredded
    mozzarella cheese
1/2 cup grated Parmesan cheese
2 eggs, lightly beaten
1 tablespoon freshly minced garlic
1/4 teaspoon freshly
    grated nutmeg
Salt and freshly ground pepper
    to taste
8 to 10 lasagna noodles,
    cooked al dente
2 to 3 cups homemade or
    good-quality tomato
    pasta sauce
Grated Parmesan cheese
    for garnish

Preheat the oven to 375 degrees. Combine the spinach, ricotta cheese, mozzarella cheese, 1/2 cup Parmesan cheese, eggs, garlic, nutmeg, salt and pepper in a bowl and mix well. Place the cooked lasagna noodles in a single layer on a sheet of waxed paper and pat dry with paper towels. Spread about 1/4 cup of the cheese mixture evenly over each noodle. Roll up the noodles, securing with wooden picks if needed. Place seam side down in a shallow baking dish, spacing slightly apart. Pour the pasta sauce in the pan around the roll-ups. Cover loosely with foil. Bake for 25 minutes or until heated through and the sauce is bubbly. Discard any wooden picks. To serve, place 2 roll-ups on each plate with some of the pasta sauce. Garnish with Parmesan cheese.

Yield: 4 to 5 servings

Note: The lasagna noodles may be cooked ahead and refrigerated in sealable plastic bags until ready to use. This recipe is also delicious with sun-dried tomato or spinach lasagna noodles.

1994 - *A grant from the Christy-Houston Foundation funds the purchase of a state-of-the-art Angel ambulance, which acts as a mobile Neonatal Intensive Care Unit.*

Great Outdoors

chapter five

Baby BLT's

Cheese Dreams

Coleslaw

Crunchy Coleslaw

Picnic Cucumber Salad

Craisin Chicken Salad

Blackened Chicken Salad

The Yellow Porch Chicken Salad

Game Day Chili

Buttermilk Corn Sticks

White Chicken Chili with Southern Corn Bread

Oven-Baked Beans

Open-Faced Tenderloin Sandwiches

Whiskey-Grilled Baby Back Ribs

Pulled Pork Barbecue

Swett's Famous Fried Chicken

Chicken Enchiladas

Longhorn Salmon

Orange Pecan Pie

"Iroquois Steeplechase" Pie

Old-Fashioned Strawberry Shortcake

Baby BLT's

1 to 2 loaves sliced bread
1 pound bacon, crisp-cooked
    and chopped
Mayonnaise
Cherry or Roma tomatoes, sliced
Salt to taste
Shredded lettuce (leaf, Bibb
    or romaine)

Cut the bread slices into rounds with a biscuit or cookie cutter. Place in a single layer on a work surface; set aside.

Combine the bacon and enough mayonnaise to make a spreadable consistency in a bowl and mix well. Sprinkle the tomato slices lightly with salt.

Spread the bread rounds with the mayonnaise mixture. Top each with a pinch of shredded lettuce, pressing lightly into the mayonnaise. Place a tomato slice on top of each. Serve immediately or chill, covered, until ready to serve.

Note: Small homegrown tomatoes may also be used. You may cut the bread into shapes using different cookie cutters. Keep the bread shapes in sealable plastic bags until ready to use.

Photo on page 133.

Yield: (about) 20 servings

Cheese Dreams

8 ounces sharp Cheddar cheese, cut
    into cubes
1 (1/4-inch-thick) onion slice
2 tablespoons mayonnaise
1 tablespoon prepared mustard
1 teaspoon Worcestershire sauce
1/4 teaspoon Tabasco sauce
Crackers or bread rounds

Combine the cheese, onion, mayonnaise, mustard, Worcestershire sauce and Tabasco sauce in a food processor and process until a spreadable consistency. Spread over crackers and serve.

Note: This cheese spread can also be used to make great grilled cheese sandwiches.

Yield: 4 to 6 servings

1994 - *Researchers at the hospital determine there is no difference in fecal contamination in cloth versus disposable diapers.*

Coleslaw

1 head green cabbage,
    finely shredded
2 large carrots, finely shredded
3/4 cup best-quality mayonnaise
2 tablespoons sugar, or to taste
2 tablespoons grated Spanish onion
2 tablespoons sour cream
2 tablespoons white vinegar
1 tablespoon dry mustard
2 teaspoons celery salt
Salt and freshly ground pepper

Combine the cabbage and carrots in a large bowl and mix well. Whisk the mayonnaise, sugar, onion, sour cream, vinegar, dry mustard, celery salt, salt and pepper in a medium bowl. Add to the cabbage mixture and mix well. Adjust the seasonings.

Yield: 6 to 8 servings

Crunchy Coleslaw

1/2 head napa cabbage, shredded
1/4 small head red cabbage, shredded
1/2 jicama, peeled, cut into thin
    strips (optional)
1 tart apple (such as Fuji, Gala,
    Braeburn, Granny Smith or
    Lady), chopped or thinly sliced
1 celery rib, thinly sliced
1/2 cup mayonnaise
1/2 cup sugar
1/4 cup milk
1/4 cup cider vinegar
3/4 teaspoon salt
1/4 teaspoon cayenne pepper

Photo on page 144.

Combine the napa cabbage, red cabbage, jicama, apple and celery in a glass bowl and toss to mix. Combine the remaining ingredients in a bowl. Drizzle 1/4 to 1/2 cup of the dressing over the cabbage mixture and toss to mix. Chill, covered, until serving time.

Note: Jicama can be found in most large supermarkets and specialty grocery stores. It has a fresh flavor and very crunchy texture. It tastes like a cross between an apple and potato.

Yield: 6 servings

FRESH PINK LEMONADE

Roll 24 lemons gently on a carving board. Cut each lemon in half and squeeze the juice from each half using a citrus juicer. Strain to remove any seeds. Pour 4 cups of boiling water into a glass gallon container. Add 2 cups sugar and stir until sugar is dissolved. Add the lemon juice and 8 cups cold water. Rinse and remove the caps from 1 pint of strawberries. Cut each strawberry in half and push the halves through a sieve, mashing with the back of a small spoon. Pour the strained strawberries into the lemonade, scraping the underside of the sieve. Stir until blended. Chill until ready to serve. Garnish with fresh mint and lemon. Omit the strawberries for traditional lemonade.

1994 - *The Junior League of Nashville establishes the Respite Care Center for weekend care of chronically ill children, giving home caregivers a rest.*

135

Picnic Cucumber Salad

2 cucumbers, peeled and sliced
1 small red onion, sliced into rings
1/2 cup cider vinegar
1/4 cup vegetable oil
1/4 teaspoon salt
Dash of freshly ground pepper

Combine the cucumbers and onion in a bowl. Add the vinegar, oil, salt and pepper and mix well. Refrigerate, covered, for several hours before serving.

Yield: 4 to 6 servings

Craisin Chicken Salad

SALAD
6 chicken breast halves, cooked
    and diced, warm
1 pound bacon, crisp-cooked
    and crumbled, warm
1 head each red leaf lettuce, green
    leaf lettuce and iceberg lettuce,
    torn into bite-size pieces
2 cups (8 ounces) shredded
    mozzarella cheese
6 ounces shredded Parmesan cheese
1 cup Craisins
1/2 cup sliced almonds

DRESSING
1 cup sugar
1/2 cup chopped sweet onion
1/2 cup red wine vinegar
2 teaspoons dry mustard
1 cup canola oil

For the salad, combine the warm chicken, warm bacon, red leaf lettuce, green leaf lettuce, iceberg lettuce, mozzarella cheese, Parmesan cheese, Craisins and almonds in a bowl and mix well; set aside.

For the dressing, combine the sugar, onion, vinegar and dry mustard in a blender and process until smooth. Add the canola oil gradually, processing constantly at high speed until well mixed. Pour over the salad and toss to mix, or serve the dressing on the side.

Yield: 4 to 6 servings

1994 - The Pediatric Emergency Department, funded by a grant from Friends of Vanderbilt Children's Hospital, is dedicated exclusively to caring for children under the age of 18.

Blackened Chicken Salad

3 cups chopped tomatoes
1 yellow bell pepper, chopped
3 tablespoons cider vinegar
1 teaspoon onion powder
1/4 teaspoon salt
1/8 teaspoon pepper
1/4 cup lemon juice
1/4 cup Dijon mustard
3 tablespoons water
1 tablespoon honey
1 pound boneless skinless chicken
    breast halves
3 tablespoons spicy seasoning
1 pound sugar snap peas, ends
    trimmed and strings removed
8 cups torn romaine lettuce

Combine the tomatoes, bell pepper, vinegar, onion powder, salt and pepper in a medium bowl and toss to mix. Refrigerate, covered, until chilled.

Whisk the lemon juice, Dijon mustard, water and honey in a medium bowl until well mixed. Refrigerate, covered, until chilled.

Rinse the chicken and pat dry. Rub generously with the spicy seasoning. Spray a large heavy skillet with nonstick cooking spray. Heat over medium-high heat until hot. Add the chicken. Cook for 7 minutes per side or until the chicken is cooked through. Remove from the skillet. Let stand until cool. Cut the chicken into bite-size pieces; set aside.

Steam the sugar snap peas for 2 minutes. Rinse under cold water; drain. Place in a large bowl with the romaine lettuce. Add the lemon juice mixture and toss to coat.

Divide the romaine mixture among 4 to 6 serving plates. Top with equal portions of the tomato mixture and chicken.

Yield: 4 to 6 servings

The Yellow Porch Chicken Salad

CHEESE WAFERS

Heat 3 sticks of butter in a bowl in the microwave until boiling. Combine 2^1/$_2$ cups unbleached flour, ^{1}/$_3$ teaspoon cayenne pepper and 1^1/$_2$ pounds finely shredded sharp Cheddar cheese in a bowl and mix well. Add the melted butter and mix well. Drop small balls onto an ungreased baking sheet, using a melon ball scooper. Cover with waxed paper and flatten the balls using the bottom of a glass. Remove the waxed paper and bake in a 350-degree oven for 30 minutes. Makes about 4 dozen cheese wafers.

5 pounds poached chicken,
   cut into bite-size pieces
1^1/$_2$ cups chopped tomatoes
^{1}/$_2$ bunch celery, chopped
^{1}/$_2$ red onion, chopped
1 cup mayonnaise
^{1}/$_2$ cup toasted walnuts
^{1}/$_2$ cup sour cream
^{1}/$_4$ cup chopped fresh herbs (such as
   basil, thyme and parsley)
Salt and pepper to taste

Combine the chicken, tomatoes, celery, onion, mayonnaise, walnuts, sour cream, herbs, salt and pepper in a bowl and mix well.

Note: Recipe may be cut in half.

Yield: 16 to 20 servings

1994 - *The hospital acquires the Angel IV ambulance, which can safely transport two infants.*

Game Day Chili

2 pounds ground beef
1 onion, chopped
1 large green bell pepper, chopped
2 garlic cloves, finely chopped
1 (15-ounce) can chili beans
1 (15-ounce) can dark red
    kidney beans
1 (15-ounce) can whole tomatoes
1 (15-ounce) can tomato sauce
3/4 cup water
1 small jalapeño chile, seeded
    and chopped
2 teaspoons chili powder
1 teaspoon each cumin and paprika
Salt and pepper to taste
Shredded cheese

Brown the ground beef in a skillet, stirring until crumbly; drain. Add the onion, bell pepper and garlic. Sauté until tender. Add the undrained chili beans, undrained kidney beans, tomatoes, tomato sauce, water, jalapeño chile, chili powder, cumin, paprika, salt and pepper and mix well. Simmer for 2 hours, stirring occasionally. Ladle into soup bowls and top with a small amount of shredded cheese. Serve with crackers.

Yield: 6 to 8 servings

Buttermilk Corn Sticks

1 1/3 cups cornmeal
1/3 cup flour
1 tablespoon sugar
1 teaspoon baking powder
1/2 teaspoon baking soda
1/2 teaspoon salt
1 cup buttermilk
1 egg, beaten
2 tablespoons shortening, melted

Preheat the oven to 400 degrees. Combine the cornmeal, flour, sugar, baking powder, baking soda and salt in a bowl and mix well. Add the buttermilk and egg and stir until the dry ingredients are moistened. Stir in the shortening. Place a well-greased cast-iron corn stick pan in the oven for 3 minutes or until hot. Remove the pan from the oven. Spoon the batter into the pan, filling 2/3 full. Bake for 12 to 15 minutes or until lightly browned.

Yield: 15 corn sticks

White Chicken Chili with Southern Corn Bread

Have you ever gone on a picnic only to discover that you've forgotten something important like the corkscrew for the wine?

Always pack in something sturdy, not plastic bags. A basket is perfect, especially one you can also use as a tabletop.

Bring a plastic tablecloth to put the food on. That way if there is an unexpected spill, you can just wipe it up. Also, consider a cheap, disposable plastic cloth on top of a blanket. When you are finished eating, you can throw the plastic cloth away and still use your blanket for that much-needed post-picnic nap!

1 onion, chopped
1 tablespoon olive oil
3 (4-ounce) cans chopped
    green chiles
2 tablespoons cumin
1 tablespoon flour
3 cups cooked Great Northern beans
1 1/2 cups chicken broth
3 cups chopped cooked chicken
Southern Corn Bread (below)

Photo on page 141.

Sauté the onion in the olive oil in a stockpot until translucent. Add the green chiles, cumin and flour. Cook for 2 minutes, stirring constantly. Stir in the beans and chicken broth. Bring to a boil. Reduce the heat to low. Simmer for 10 minutes. Add the chicken. Simmer for 10 minutes. Serve with Southern Corn Bread.

Yield: 6 servings

Southern Corn Bread

2 cups cornmeal
1 tablespoon baking powder
1 teaspoon salt
1 teaspoon sugar
3 eggs
1 1/4 cups milk
1 1/4 cups vegetable oil

Preheat the oven to 425 degrees. Grease a cast-iron skillet or loaf pan and heat in the oven.

Sift the cornmeal, baking powder, salt and sugar together; set aside. Beat the eggs with a fork in a bowl. Stir in the milk and oil. Add the cornmeal mixture and beat until well blended. Pour into the hot skillet. Bake for 15 to 20 minutes or until the corn bread tests done.

Yield: 8 servings

  **1995 -** *A new technique that speeds up the process of stripping toxic ammonia from the blood of newborns is pioneered.*

Oven-Baked Beans

ICED TEA

Boil 2 cups sugar with 2 cups water in a saucepan for 5 minutes. Steep 8 single-serving tea bags in 1 quart of hot water for 5 minutes. Remove the tea bags. Combine the sugar water, tea and 2 quarts of cold water in a pitcher. Refrigerate until chilled. Stir in 2 cups orange juice and 3/4 cup lemon juice. Garnish with orange or lemon slices.

2 cups dried kidney beans
1 (8-ounce) can tomato sauce
4 ounces salt pork or thick
    bacon, sliced
1/2 cup chopped onion
1 tablespoon molasses
1 teaspoon parsley
1/2 teaspoon salt
Dash of pepper

Sort and rinse the beans. Combine the beans and enough water to cover in a bowl. Soak, covered, for 8 to 12 hours.

Preheat the oven to 300 degrees. Drain the beans. Place in a Dutch oven or baking dish large enough to allow for the beans to swell during cooking. Add enough water to cover the beans. Stir in the tomato sauce, salt pork, onion, molasses, parsley, salt and pepper. Bake, covered, for 2 1/2 hours. Check the beans and add a little more water if necessary. Bake for 1 hour longer or until the beans are tender.

Note: These beans pair well with hot water corn cakes.

Yield: 6 to 8 servings

1995 - The Matthew Albert Tucker Research Fund for pediatric brain injury is established to research brain cell injuries and how families cope with stress after discharge.

Open-Faced Tenderloin Sandwiches

1 (2-pound) beef tenderloin, trimmed

Salt and pepper to taste

1 (14-ounce) can artichoke
    hearts, drained

1 cup mayonnaise

1/2 cup (2 ounces) grated
    Parmesan cheese

1 to 2 garlic cloves

2 loaves French bread, cut into
    1/4-inch slices

Spinach leaves

Roasted red bell pepper, sliced

Preheat the oven to 400 degrees. Season the tenderloin with salt and pepper. Place the tenderloin fat side up on a rack in a roasting pan. Roast to 140 degrees on a meat thermometer. Tent with foil and let stand until cool. Carve into slices.

Combine the artichoke hearts, mayonnaise, cheese and garlic in a blender or food processor and process until puréed.

Spread the artichoke purée over the bread slices. Top with spinach, red peppers and sliced beef.

Yield: 8 servings

Going early to the game to tailgate with some friends? Here are some tips that will make your meal extra special!

Make sure the grill is hot enough before starting to cook, and always grill the meat and veggies about four inches from the heat source.

Presoaking natural hardwoods such as hickory adds extra flavor to your food. Close the top of the grill, and let the food soak in some of the smoky flavor.

1995 - *The National Cancer Institute chooses the Hematology/Oncology Clinic as one of 17 sites worldwide for Phase 1 trials of experimental cancer drugs for children.*

 143

1995 - *The Junior League Asthma Center opens.*

Whiskey-Grilled Baby Back Ribs

3 (2-pound) racks baby back
    pork ribs
Salt and coarsely ground black
    pepper to taste
1 tablespoon ground red
    chile pepper
Whiskey Sauce (below)

Preheat the oven to 300 degrees. Cut each rack of ribs into halves. Sprinkle with salt, black pepper and red chile pepper. Wrap each half rack in foil. Place on a baking sheet. Bake for about 3 hours. Preheat the grill. Unwrap the ribs and discard the foil. Place on a grill rack over hot coals. Brush generously with Whiskey Sauce. Grill for 5 to 10 minutes per side, brushing frequently with the sauce. Serve immediately with additional sauce.

Note: These ribs are delicious served with Crunchy Coleslaw (page 135).

Photo on page 144.

Yield: 6 to 8 servings

Whiskey Sauce

1 cup water
1/2 cup minced onion
1/2 cup packed brown sugar
1/2 cup tomato sauce
1/2 cup white wine vinegar
1/4 cup whiskey
3 tablespoons Worcestershire sauce
2 1/2 tablespoons honey
2 1/4 tablespoons vegetable oil
1 1/2 tablespoons molasses
1 tablespoon garlic powder
2 teaspoons salt
1/2 teaspoon each coarsely ground
    black pepper, paprika, onion
    powder and red pepper flakes

Combine the water, onion, brown sugar, tomato sauce, vinegar, whiskey, Worcestershire sauce, honey, oil, molasses, garlic powder, salt, black pepper, paprika, onion powder and pepper flakes in a heavy saucepan, mixing well after each addition. Bring to a boil over medium-high heat. Reduce the heat. Simmer for 1 1/2 to 2 hours or until thickened, stirring occasionally. Remove from the heat; cover and set aside until ready to use.

Note: This sauce is also delicious on grilled chicken.

Pulled Pork Barbecue

Trying to figure out serving portions can be frustrating. To help, remember that meat loses about 25 percent of its weight during cooking. Four ounces uncooked will yield about 3 ounces cooked. To make ground meat even healthier, brown it and then place in a colander lined with paper towels. Allow the fat to drain. Buy only the leanest cuts of beef, pork, and turkey. Prepackaged ground beef is generally higher in fat than non-ground beef. Ask the butcher to grind a sirloin steak and have him remove all visible fat.

PORK

3 tablespoons coarse sea salt

3 tablespoons paprika

1 tablespoon garlic powder

1 tablespoon dry mustard

1 tablespoon brown sugar

1 (5- to 7-pound) pork shoulder or
  Boston butt

BARBECUE SAUCE

1 1/2 cups cider vinegar

1 cup yellow or brown mustard

1/2 cup ketchup

1/3 cup packed brown sugar

2 garlic cloves, crushed

1 teaspoon kosher salt

1 teaspoon cayenne pepper

1/2 teaspoon freshly ground
  black pepper

ASSEMBLY

3/4 cup water

For the pork, combine the sea salt, paprika, garlic powder, dry mustard and brown sugar in a small bowl and mix well. Rub over the entire surface of the pork. Refrigerate, covered, for 1 to 12 hours.

Preheat the oven to 300 degrees. Place the pork fat side up on a rack in a roasting pan. Roast for 6 hours or until a meat thermometer registers 170 degrees and the pork is falling apart.

For the barbecue sauce, combine the vinegar, yellow mustard, ketchup, brown sugar, garlic, kosher salt, cayenne pepper and black pepper in a saucepan. Simmer over medium heat for 10 minutes, stirring frequently. Remove from the heat and set aside.

To assemble, place the pork on a serving platter; set aside. Place the roasting pan over medium heat. Add the water and stir with a wooden spoon to deglaze the pan. Pour into the barbecue sauce. Cook for 5 minutes or until heated through. Serve with the pork.

Yield: 12 servings

Swett's Famous Fried Chicken

1 egg
1/2 cup water
1 teaspoon salt
1 teaspoon garlic powder
1 teaspoon cracked pepper
4 cups flour
1 teaspoon salt
1 teaspoon garlic powder
1 teaspoon ground pepper
1 (3-pound) chicken, cut into
    8 pieces
Vegetable oil for frying

Combine the egg, water, 1 teaspoon salt, 1 teaspoon garlic powder and cracked pepper in a bowl and mix well; set aside. Combine the flour, 1 teaspoon salt, 1 teaspoon garlic powder and ground pepper in a bowl and mix well.

Rinse the chicken and pat dry. Dip in the egg mixture. Coat with the seasoned flour. Let stand for a few minues or until dry. Coat the chicken in the seasoned flour again. Heat oil to 325 degrees in a fryer or skillet. Fry the chicken in the oil until golden brown and a meat thermometer registers 180 degrees. Drain on paper towels.

Yield: 4 to 6 servings

Chicken Enchiladas

2 cups chopped cooked chicken
1 cup sour cream
2 cups (8 ounces) shredded Colby
    and Monterey Jack cheese blend
1 cup salsa
2 tablespoons chopped fresh cilantro
1 teaspoon cumin
10 (6-inch) flour tortillas
1 cup shredded lettuce
1/2 cup chopped tomato

Preheat the oven to 350 degrees. Combine the chicken, sour cream, 1 cup of the cheese, 1/4 cup of the salsa, cilantro and cumin in a bowl and mix well. Spoon 1/4 cup of the chicken mixture down the center of each tortilla; roll up to enclose the filling. Place seam side down in a 9×13-inch baking dish. Top with the remaining 3/4 cup salsa.

Bake for 30 minutes. Sprinkle with the remaining 1 cup cheese. Bake for 5 minutes or until the cheese is melted. Top with the lettuce and tomato. Serve with additional sour cream.

Yield: 4 to 6 servings

Longhorn Salmon

2 (8-ounce) salmon fillets,
   skin removed
$1/2$ cup vegetable oil
$1/4$ cup pineapple juice
2 tablespoons packed brown sugar
2 tablespoons soy sauce
1 teaspoon bourbon
$1/2$ teaspoon pepper
$1/8$ teaspoon garlic powder
2 teaspoons chopped fresh chives

Place the salmon fillets in a baking dish. Combine the oil, pineapple juice, brown sugar, soy sauce, bourbon, pepper and garlic powder in a bowl and mix well. Pour over the salmon. Marinate, covered, in the refrigerator for 1 to 12 hours.

Preheat the grill or broiler. Remove the salmon from the marinade, reserving the marinade. Grill or broil the salmon for 5 to 7 minutes per side or until the fish flakes easily, brushing with the reserved marinade only during the first 5 minutes of cooking. Sprinkle with the chives.

Yield: 2 to 4 servings

1996 - The name Children's Hospital at Vanderbilt University Medical Center is officially changed to Vanderbilt Children's Hospital.

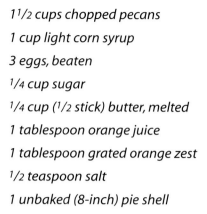

Orange Pecan Pie

1¹/2 cups chopped pecans
1 cup light corn syrup
3 eggs, beaten
¹/4 cup sugar
¹/4 cup (¹/2 stick) butter, melted
1 tablespoon orange juice
1 tablespoon grated orange zest
¹/2 teaspoon salt
1 unbaked (8-inch) pie shell

Preheat the oven to 350 degrees. Combine the pecans, corn syrup, eggs, sugar, butter, orange juice, orange zest and salt in a bowl and mix well. Pour into the pie shell. Bake for 45 minutes or until the center is set. Cool on a wire rack. Serve warm or at room temperature.

Note: With just a hint of orange to enhance the flavor, this pie is great for the holidays.

Yield: 1 (8-inch) pie

"Iroquois Steeplechase" Pie

¹/2 cup flour
¹/2 cup granulated sugar
¹/2 cup packed brown sugar
2 eggs
1 cup (2 sticks) butter or margarine
1 cup (6 ounces) semisweet
    chocolate chips
1 cup walnuts
1 unbaked (9-inch) pie shell
8 ounces whipped topping

Preheat the oven to 375 degrees. Combine the flour, granulated sugar, brown sugar and eggs in a bowl and mix well; set aside. Melt the butter in a saucepan. Remove from the heat. Let cool for about 5 minutes. Stir in the chocolate chips and walnuts. Add to the flour mixture. Pour into the pie shell. Bake for 30 to 35 minutes or until set. Serve warm with the whipped topping.

Yield: 1 (9-inch) pie

"IROQUOIS STEEPLECHASE" MINT JULEP

Cover 10 to 12 fresh mint leaves with 1 teaspoon confectioners' sugar in a bowl. Add a few drops of water and muddle. Remove half of the muddled mint and place in a silver julep glass. Top with enough crushed ice to fill the glass half full. Add 1 jigger Tennessee whiskey and 1 jigger apricot schnapps. Add the remaining muddled mint. Fill remainder of glass with crushed ice. Stir with a long spoon until frost appears on the outside of the glass. Rub the rim of the glass with lime. Garnish with fruit and mint.

1996 - The Memorial Foundation Inc. of Goodlettsville grant is used to conduct research on new childhood vaccines.

Old-Fashioned Strawberry Shortcake

Always set your timer 10 minutes before the recommended cooking time is up. You can always add additional baking time, but once something is burned, there is no turning back the clock.

2 cups flour
1 cup granulated sugar
1 teaspoon baking powder
1/2 teaspoon salt
1/2 cup (1 stick) butter
2 eggs
Sliced strawberries to taste
Granulated sugar to taste
1 cup whipping cream
1/4 cup confectioners' sugar
Fresh mint sprig for garnish

Preheat the oven to 350 degrees. Line an 8-inch round cake pan with waxed paper.

Combine the flour, 1 cup granulated sugar, baking powder and salt in a bowl and mix well. Cut in the butter until crumbly. Add the eggs and stir just until the dry ingredients are moistened. Turn the dough out onto a lightly floured surface. Knead gently several times to form a ball. (Dough will be slightly grainy.) Press evenly into the prepared pan. Bake for 35 minutes or until the shortcake tests done. Cool on a wire rack.

Combine strawberries and granulated sugar to taste in a bowl and mix well. Beat the cream with the confectioners' sugar in a bowl until soft peaks form. Split the shortcake horizontally into 2 even layers. Fill the layers with half the whipped cream and strawberries. Top with the remaining whipped cream and strawberries. Garnish with the mint.

Photo on page 151.

Yield: 1 (8-inch) cake

Children's Favorites

chapter six

Bird's Nests

Aron's Pimento Cheese

All-I-Want-for-Lunch Grilled Cheese Sandwich

Once-a-Year Macaroni and Cheese

Chicken Potpie

Spaghetti Casserole

Pizza Mini Me's

Caramel Corn

Caramel Apples

Peach Cobbler

Homemade Lemon Ice Cream

Chocolate Cupcakes with Frosting

Karyn's Spice Cake

Hot Fudge Pudding

Fudgy Brownies

Nanaimo Bars II

KK's Chocolate Chip Cookies

Friends Favorite Sugar Cookies

Super Sugar Cookies

Mother's Snowflakes

Chocolate Peanut Butter Bonbons

Chocolate-Dipped Treats

Fudge

SMOOTHIE

Process 1 banana, 1 cup frozen unsweetened strawberries, 1 cup vanilla yogurt and 1/2 cup milk in a blender until smooth. For a pretty look, drop a few fresh berries into the bottom of the glass. Pour the smoothie into the glass. If you freeze the banana in advance it will make the smoothie colder.

Bird's Nests

4 thick slices Italian bread
2 tablespoons butter, softened
4 eggs

Cut a hole from the center of each bread slice with a cookie or biscuit cutter. Spread both sides of the bread slices with the butter. Place in a skillet over medium heat. Carefully crack 1 egg into the hole in each bread slice. Cook until the egg whites turn milky and opaque. Turn over carefully so the egg yolks don't break. Continue cooking until the egg whites are set and the egg yolks begin to thicken. Serve immediately.

Photo on page 155.

Yield: 4 servings

Aron's Pimento Cheese

2 cups (8 ounces) shredded sharp
    Cheddar cheese
2 cups (8 ounces) finely shredded
    sharp Cheddar cheese
1 to 1 1/2 cups mayonnaise
1 (4-ounce) jar pimentos, drained
1/4 cup fresh parsley, finely chopped
Pepper to taste

Combine the cheeses, mayonnaise, pimentos, parsley and pepper in a bowl and mix well. Chill, covered, for 8 to 12 hours.

Yield: 8 to 10 servings

1998 - A new Angel ambulance is purchased for the transportation of infants.

155

All-I-Want-for-Lunch Grilled Cheese Sandwich

2 slices Cheddar, American or
    Swiss cheese
2 slices white bread
2 tablespoons butter, softened

Place the cheese between the bread slices. Melt 1 tablespoon of the butter in a skillet. Add the sandwich. Cook until golden brown, gently pressing down with a spatula. Add the remaining butter; turn over the sandwich. Cook until golden brown.

Note: You may also top the cheese with any of the following before cooking: 3 slices bacon, cooked (not crisp) and drained; 2 thin slices ham; or 2 thin slices tomato.

Yield: 1 serving

Once-a-Year Macaroni and Cheese

16 ounces rotini or elbow macaroni
11 to 12 cups (2³/4 to 3 pounds)
    sharp Cheddar cheese, shredded
3 tablespoons flour
2 teaspoons salt
2 teaspoons dry mustard
¹/2 teaspoon black pepper
¹/4 teaspoon each nutmeg and
    cayenne pepper or chipotle
    chili pepper
2¹/4 cups half-and-half
1³/4 cups heavy cream
1¹/3 cups sour cream
3 eggs, beaten
1¹/2 teaspoons Worcestershire sauce

Preheat the oven to 350 degrees. Cook the rotini according to the package directions until al dente; drain. Place in a buttered 9×13-inch baking dish. Add 8 cups of the cheese and toss to mix; set aside.

Combine the flour, salt, dry mustard, black pepper, nutmeg and cayenne pepper in a mixing bowl and mix well. Beat in the half-and-half, cream, sour cream, eggs and Worcestershire sauce. Pour over the rotini mixture. Sprinkle the remaining 3 to 4 cups cheese over the top.

Bake for 45 minutes or until the sauce is thickened around the edges. Let stand for 10 minutes before serving.

Yield: 8 to 10 servings

Photo on page 157.

1998 - Proceeds from the Davidson County Friends Holiday Project fund the playscape for the Orthopedic Clinic.

157

Chicken Potpie

1/4 cup (1/2 stick) butter
5 tablespoons flour
1/2 cup madeira or dry sherry
2 1/2 cups chicken stock
1 teaspoon chopped fresh thyme
1/2 teaspoon salt
1/4 teaspoon freshly ground pepper
1 cup heavy cream or half-and-half
6 cups chopped cooked chicken
1 cup frozen peas
1 cup shredded carrots
1 (17-ounce) package frozen
*   puff pastry*
1 egg

Photo on page 157.

Preheat the oven to 400 degrees. Melt the butter in a 4-quart saucepan. Whisk in the flour. Cook for 2 minutes or until bubbly, whisking constantly. Add the madeira. Add the chicken stock gradually, whisking constantly. Cook for 4 to 6 minutes or until thickened and smooth, whisking constantly. Stir in the thyme, salt and pepper. Add the cream gradually, stirring constantly. Stir in the chicken, peas and carrots. Cook for 20 minutes. Divide evenly among 6 to 8 individual ovenproof bowls.

Meanwhile, thaw the puff pastry according to the package directions. Unfold 1 pastry sheet at a time on a lightly floured surface. Roll out slightly. Repeat with the remaining pastry. Cut 3 to 4 circles from each pastry sheet in a diameter slightly larger than the bowls. Moisten the edge of each circle with water and drape over the top of a bowl, sealing or fluting the edge. Cut out decorative shapes, such as leaves, from the pastry scraps with a sharp knife if desired. Brush the cutouts with water and gently press on top. Cut vents in the top pastry. Place the bowls on a baking sheet. Combine the egg with a small amount of water in a bowl and mix well. Brush over the tops of the potpies. Bake for 10 minutes. Reduce the oven temperature to 350 degrees and bake for 40 minutes.

Yield: 6 to 8 servings

1998 - *Doctors treat 17,000 children at the new pediatric emergency department, which offers a completely separate child-oriented environment.*

Spaghetti Casserole

4 tablespoons canola oil

2 pounds ground round

2 onions, minced

2 celery ribs, minced

1 garlic clove, minced

3 (15-ounce) cans tomato sauce

3 bay leaves

1 to 1¹/₂ teaspoons salt

2 dashes of thyme

Dash of cayenne pepper

8 ounces mushrooms, sliced

Butter

1 to 1¹/₂ zucchini, cut lengthwise
    into quarters and sliced

2 yellow squash, cut lengthwise
    into quarters and sliced

8 ounces (or more) angel hair pasta

2 cups (8 ounces) shredded sharp
    Cheddar cheese

Heat 2 tablespoons of the canola oil in a skillet. Brown the ground round in the oil, stirring until crumbly; drain. Remove to a bowl; set aside.

Heat the remaining 2 tablespoons canola oil in the same skillet. Add the onions, celery and garlic. Sauté until the onions are translucent. Remove to a Dutch oven. Stir in the ground round, tomato sauce, bay leaves, salt, thyme and cayenne pepper. Simmer for 1 to 1¹/₂ hours, stirring occasionally.

Meanwhile, sauté the mushrooms in a skillet in a small amount of butter and water. Steam the zucchini and yellow squash in a steamer just until tender. Cook the angel hair pasta according to the package directions; drain.

Preheat the oven to 350 degrees. Remove and discard the bay leaves from the sauce. Add the mushrooms, zucchini, yellow squash and angel hair pasta and stir to evenly distribute the sauce. Spoon into a 9×13-inch baking dish. Sprinkle with the cheese.

Bake, covered, for 20 minutes. Bake, uncovered, until the top is lightly browned and the liquid is reduced.

Note: This is a great recipe for a crowd.

Yield: 12 servings

Pizza Mini Me's

1 (8-ounce) can tomato sauce
1 teaspoon sugar
1/4 teaspoon Italian seasoning
1/4 teaspoon dried minced onion
1/8 teaspoon garlic powder
3 English muffins, split and
    lightly toasted
18 thin slices pepperoni (optional)
1/2 cup (2 ounces) shredded
    mozzarella cheese
1 1/2 teaspoons grated
    Parmesan cheese

Preheat the oven to 400 degrees. Combine the tomato sauce, sugar, Italian seasoning, onion and garlic powder in a small heavy saucepan and mix well. Bring to a boil. Simmer for 3 to 4 minutes, stirring frequently.

Spread each English muffin half with about 1 tablespoon of the sauce. Arrange 3 pepperoni slices on top of the sauce. Sprinkle with 4 teaspoons of the mozzarella cheese and 1/4 teaspoon of the Parmesan cheese. Place the pizzas on a baking sheet. Bake for 3 1/2 minutes.

Yield: 6 servings

Caramel Corn

6 cups popped popcorn
3 tablespoons butter
1/4 cup light corn syrup
1 tablespoon molasses

Preheat the oven to 325 degrees. Place the popcorn in a baking sheet with a rim; set aside. Melt the butter in a saucepan over low heat. Remove from the heat. Stir in the corn syrup and molasses and blend well. Pour evenly over the popcorn. Toss with a wooden spoon until evenly coated.

Bake for 15 minutes, stirring with a wooden spoon every 5 minutes. Remove to waxed paper. Let stand until cool. Store in an airtight container.

Yield: 6 cups

1998 - Children from Middle Tennessee create buttons for a mosaic art project honoring the 25th anniversary of the hospital.

Caramel Apples

12 tart apples

12 wooden popsicle sticks

1 cup (2 sticks) unsalted butter

2¹/4 cups packed brown sugar

2 cups light cream

1 cup light corn syrup

1 teaspoon vanilla extract

1 cup chopped walnuts, pecans or
   peanuts (optional)

Rinse the apples and pat dry; remove and discard the stems. Insert a wooden popsicle stick into the stem end of each apple. Place on a buttered baking sheet; set aside.

Melt the butter in a heavy 3-quart saucepan over low heat. Add the brown sugar, cream and corn syrup. Bring to a boil over medium-high heat, stirring constantly. Reduce the heat to medium. Cook to 248 degrees on a candy thermometer, firm-ball stage, stirring constantly. Remove from the heat. Stir in the vanilla. Dip 1 apple at a time into the hot caramel, turning to coat completely. Dip the bottom of the coated apples into the walnuts. May stripe apples with white chocolate or semi-sweet chocolate. Return to the baking sheet. Chill until the caramel is set.

Photo on page 153.

Yield: 12 servings

What child doesn't like to play with playdough? What could be more fun than being able to eat your playdough? Here's a recipe that's sure to be fun to make AND eat. Knead ¹/2 cup peanut butter, ¹/2 cup honey, and 1 cup powdered milk together.

1998 - *Vanderbilt Children's Hospital receives the state's highest level designation as a comprehensive regional pediatric center.*

 161

Peach Cobbler

HONEY SPICE SNAPS

Sift together 2¹/4 cups flour, ¹/2 teaspoon salt, ¹/2 teaspoon ground cinnamon, 1¹/2 teaspoons baking soda, ¹/4 teaspoon ground cloves and 1 teaspoon ground ginger into a bowl. Cream 1 cup firmly packed brown sugar with ³/4 cup shortening in a bowl. Beat in 1 egg and ¹/4 cup honey. Add the sifted dry ingredients and mix well. Roll the dough into balls using a teaspoon. Dip half of each ball into water, then into sugar. Place sugar side up on a greased cookie sheet. Bake in a 350-degree oven for 12 to 15 minutes.

4¹/2 cups sliced peeled peaches
¹/4 cup sugar
¹/3 teaspoon ground cinnamon
1 cup flour
¹/2 cup sugar
¹/2 cup (1 stick) cold butter, cut into pieces
Vanilla ice cream (optional)

Preheat the oven to 375 degrees. Combine the peaches, ¹/4 cup sugar and cinnamon in a bowl and mix well. Spoon into a greased 2-quart rectangular baking dish. Combine the flour, ¹/2 cup sugar and butter in a food processor and process until crumbly. Sprinkle over the peaches. Bake for about 35 minutes. Serve with ice cream.

Yield: 6 to 8 servings

Homemade Lemon Ice Cream

4 lemons, very thinly sliced
Juice of 5 lemons
2¹/2 cups sugar
2 quarts half-and-half
1 quart heavy cream
³/4 cup sugar

Combine the lemon slices, lemon juice and 2¹/2 cups sugar in a bowl and mix well. Let stand, covered, for 8 to 12 hours.

Add the half-and-half, heavy cream and ³/4 cup sugar to the lemon mixture and mix well. Refrigerate, covered, until chilled. Pour into an ice cream freezer container. Freeze according to the manufacturer's instructions.

Photo on page 163.

Yield: 1¹/2 gallons

1998 - Children's Hospital staff grows to include 103 board-certified physicians.

Chocolate Cupcakes with Frosting

1 1/2 cups (9 ounces) semisweet
    chocolate chips
1 (1-pound) package brown sugar
1/2 cup (1 stick) butter, softened
3 eggs
2 cups flour
1 teaspoon baking soda
1/2 teaspoon salt
1 cup sour cream
1 cup hot water
2 teaspoons vanilla extract
Chocolate Frosting (below)

Preheat the oven to 350 degrees. Place the chocolate chips in a microwave-safe bowl. Microwave on High for 1 minute or until melted; set aside.

Beat the brown sugar and butter at medium speed in a mixing bowl for 5 minutes or until well blended. Add the eggs 1 at a time, beating well after each addition. Beat in the melted chocolate. Sift the flour, baking soda and salt together. Add to the chocolate batter alternately with the sour cream, beating at low speed until blended after each addition. Add the hot water in a slow, steady stream, beating constantly at low speed. Stir in the vanilla.

Fill 36 paper-lined muffin cups 2/3 full with batter. Bake for 18 minutes or until a wooden pick inserted into the center of a cupcake comes out clean. Cool completely on a wire rack. Frost the cupcakes with the Chocolate Frosting.

Yield: 3 dozen cupcakes

Chocolate Frosting

4 ounces unsweetened chocolate
3 tablespoons margarine
3 cups sifted confectioners' sugar
7 tablespoons milk
1 teaspoon vanilla extract
1/8 teaspoon salt

Melt the chocolate and margarine in a double boiler over simmering water; stir until smooth.

Combine the confectioners' sugar, milk, vanilla and salt in a bowl and stir until blended. Add the chocolate mixture and mix well. Let stand until the mixture is a spreadable consistency, stirring occasionally.

Karyn's Spice Cake

2 cups granulated sugar
1 cup vegetable oil
3 eggs
2 (4-ounce) jars apricot baby food
2 cups flour
1 teaspoon baking soda
1 teaspoon ground cinnamon
1 teaspoon grated nutmeg
1/2 teaspoon salt
Confectioners' sugar for dusting
   (optional)

Preheat the oven to 350 degrees. Beat the granulated sugar and oil in a mixing bowl until well blended. Add the eggs 1 at a time, mixing well after each addition. Beat in the baby food. Add the flour, baking soda, cinnamon, nutmeg and salt and mix well.

Pour into a greased bundt pan. Bake for 1 hour or until the cake tests done. Cool in the pan for 10 minutes. Invert onto a serving plate. Cool completely. Dust with confectioners' sugar before serving.

Yield: 8 to 10 servings

Children LOVE picnics! Be creative when planning their menu, or more importantly, let them plan it. It doesn't matter for the day if they want peanut butter and pickle sandwiches. Let them build their own picnic feast. You might want to bring all the ingredients and let them assemble their food at the site. Bring cookie cutters to cut the sandwiches into fun shapes. Let the kids pack the basket with their favorite things to eat, even if there is not one single healthy thing in it. It's just for one meal! To them, it will be like they are breaking all the rules.

Hot Fudge Pudding

1 cup flour

3/4 cup granulated sugar

2 tablespoons baking cocoa

2 teaspoons baking powder

1/2 teaspoon salt

1/2 cup milk

2 tablespoons butter, melted

1 teaspoon vanilla extract

1/2 cup chopped nuts

1 cup packed brown sugar

1/4 cup baking cocoa

2 3/4 cups boiling water

Preheat the oven to 350 degrees. Sift the flour, granulated sugar, 2 tablespoons baking cocoa, baking powder and salt into a bowl. Add the milk, butter and vanilla and stir until smooth. Stir in the nuts. Pour into a greased 9×9-inch baking dish.

Combine the brown sugar and 1/4 cup baking cocoa in a bowl and mix well. Sprinkle over the top of the pudding mixture. Pour the boiling water evenly over the top. Bake for 35 to 40 minutes. Serve hot or cold.

Yield: 6 servings

Fudgy Brownies

1 cup (2 sticks) butter or margarine

4 ounces unsweetened chocolate

2 cups sugar

4 eggs

1 cup flour

1 teaspoon vanilla extract

1/2 teaspoon salt

2 cups coarsely chopped nuts
    (optional)

Preheat the oven to 350 degrees. Melt the butter and chocolate in a 3-quart saucepan over very low heat, stirring constantly. Remove from the heat. Stir in the sugar. Cool slightly. Add the eggs 1 at a time, beating well after each addition. Add the flour, vanilla and salt and mix well. Stir in the nuts. Pour into a greased 9×13-inch baking pan. Bake for 30 minutes or until a wooden pick inserted into the center comes out clean; do not overbake. Cool in the pan on a wire rack. Cut with a sharp knife into squares.

Yield: 16 to 20 servings

1999 - Stars of the Grand Ole Opry perform a benefit concert for the hospital.

Nanaimo Bars II

CRUST

1/2 cup (1 stick) butter
1/2 cup baking cocoa
1/4 cup sugar
1 egg, beaten
1 teaspoon vanilla extract
2 cups graham cracker crumbs
1/2 cup chopped walnuts
1/2 cup shredded coconut

FILLING

1/4 cup (1/2 stick) butter, softened
2 tablespoons vanilla instant
*   pudding mix*
2 cups confectioners' sugar
3 tablespoons milk

TOPPING

3 ounces semisweet chocolate
2 tablespoons butter
Milk

For the crust, combine the butter, baking cocoa and sugar in a double boiler. Heat over simmering water until the butter is melted, stirring constantly. Let stand until cool. Stir in the egg and vanilla. Add the graham cracker crumbs, walnuts and coconut and mix well. Press firmly over the bottom of an 8×8-inch baking pan. Refrigerate until chilled.

For the filling, cream the butter and pudding mix in a bowl. Add the confectioners' sugar and milk and beat until smooth. Spread over the crust. Chill, covered, until set.

For the topping, heat the chocolate and butter in a double boiler until melted, stirring constantly and adding a small amount of milk if needed to reach the desired consistency. Pour evenly over the filling. Refrigerate until chilled. Cut into squares.

Yield: 12 servings

KK's Chocolate Chip Cookies

All professional cooks will tell you that you must have all the ingredients assembled before you start. It simplifies the process of cooking. Have everything measured and chopped before you begin. Never start to cook before you have washed your hands!

1/2 cup (1 stick) butter, melted
1 egg
1/2 cup granulated sugar
1/2 cup packed light brown sugar
1/4 cup packed dark brown sugar
1/2 teaspoon baking soda
1/2 teaspoon salt
1/2 teaspoon vanilla extract
1 1/2 cups unbleached flour
1 cup (6 ounces) semisweet
  chocolate chips

Preheat the oven to 350 degrees. Beat the butter and egg in a mixing bowl until blended. Add the granulated sugar, light brown sugar and dark brown sugar and mix well. Stir in the baking soda, salt and vanilla. Add the flour and chocolate chips and mix well.

Scoop into 1-inch balls. Place 2 inches apart on a greased cookie sheet. Bake for about 10 minutes; do not overbake. Let cool on the cookie sheet.

Note: You may add English toffee bits to the dough with the chocolate chips.

Yield: 2 dozen cookies

Friends Favorite Sugar Cookies

1 cup (2 sticks) butter, softened
1¹/2 cups confectioners' sugar
1 egg
1 teaspoon vanilla extract
¹/2 teaspoon almond extract
2¹/2 cups unbleached flour
1 teaspoon baking soda
1 teaspoon cream of tartar
Friends Favorite Cookie Icing
    (below)

Beat the butter, confectioners' sugar, egg, vanilla extract and almond extract in a mixing bowl until well mixed. Blend in the flour, baking soda and cream of tartar. Chill, covered, for 2 to 3 hours.

Preheat the oven to 375 degrees. Divide the dough into halves. Roll each half about ¹/8 inch thick on a lightly floured surface. Cut with cookie cutters into desired shapes. Place on a parchment paper-lined cookie sheet. Bake for 7 to 8 minutes. Remove immediately to a wire rack to cool completely. Spread with Friends Favorite Cookie Icing. You may sprinkle the cookies with tinted sugar before baking and omit the icing.

Yield: 2 dozen cookies

Friends of Davidson County host three Tuesday evening events, including dinner for the patients and their families.

Friends Favorite Cookie Icing

3 egg whites, at room temperature
¹/2 teaspoon cream of tartar
5¹/2 cups sifted confectioners' sugar

Combine the egg whites and cream of tartar in a bowl. Add the confectioners' sugar gradually, mixing until smooth.

Note: If raw eggs are a problem in your area, use meringue powder and follow package instructions.

2000 - *Approximately 7,000 children are treated as inpatients.*

Super Sugar Cookies

1 cup (2 sticks) margarine, softened
    (do not use butter)
1 cup vegetable oil
1 cup granulated sugar
1 cup confectioners' sugar
2 eggs
1 teaspoon vanilla extract
4 cups flour
1 teaspoon baking soda
1 teaspoon cream of tartar
1 teaspoon salt
Granulated sugar for coating

Beat the margarine, oil and 1 cup granulated sugar in a mixing bowl until creamy. Add the confectioners' sugar, eggs and vanilla and mix well. Sift the flour, baking soda, cream of tartar and salt together. Add to the creamed mixture and mix well. Chill, covered, for at least 2 hours.

Preheat the oven to 350 degrees. Shape the dough into 1-inch balls. Coat with granulated sugar. Place 2 inches apart on a lightly greased cookie sheet and flatten. Bake for 12 minutes or until the edges are lightly browned. Cool on the cookie sheet for a few minutes. Remove to a wire rack to cool completely.

Note: These cookies freeze well.

Photo on page 170.

Yield: 100 cookies

Children getting underfoot in the summer? Tired of hearing that ol' refrain, "What can I do? I'm bored"? Let your children make their own fun bubbles. Combine 1/2 cup dish soap, such as Joy or Sunlight, with 2 tablespoons corn syrup in a container. Use commercial bubble wands or whatever is around the kitchen such as an apple corer, potato masher, hollow handles of utensils, or the like. The kids will go through this pretty fast, so get them to make an extra batch!

Mother's Snowflakes

2 egg whites, at room temperature
1/8 teaspoon salt
1/8 teaspoon cream of tartar
3/4 cup sugar
1 cup (6 ounces) semisweet
    chocolate chips
2/3 cup chopped pecans (optional)
1 teaspoon vanilla extract

Preheat the oven to 300 degrees. Beat the egg whites with the salt and cream of tartar in a mixing bowl until soft peaks form. Add the sugar gradually, beating constantly until stiff peaks form. Fold in the chocolate chips, pecans and vanilla.

Drop by rounded teaspoonfuls 2 inches apart onto parchment paper-lined cookie sheets. Bake for 25 minutes. Remove from the cookie sheets with a sharp-edged spatula. Store in an airtight container.

Yield: 2 dozen cookies

Chocolate Peanut Butter Bonbons

2 (1-pound) packages plus 1 cup
    confectioners' sugar
2 cups creamy peanut butter
2 cups (4 sticks) margarine, melted
3 tablespoons vanilla extract
1 1/2 pounds chocolate bark, melted

Combine the confectioners' sugar, peanut butter, margarine and vanilla in a mixing bowl and mix well. Chill, covered, for 4 hours.

Shape the peanut butter mixture into 1-inch balls. Place on a waxed paper-lined baking sheet. Chill, covered, for 2 hours.

Dip the bonbons into the melted chocolate bark to coat using wooden picks. Place on a waxed paper-lined baking sheet. Let stand until the chocolate is set.

Yield: 100 to 150 bonbons

Chocolate-Dipped Treats

2 cups (12 ounces) semisweet
　　chocolate chips
20 cherries with stems
20 strawberries with stems
10 graham crackers, broken
　　into quarters
10 small pretzels

Line 2 baking sheets with foil or parchment paper; set aside. Melt the chocolate chips in a double boiler over simmering water for about 5 minutes, stirring constantly. Do not let the chocolate become too hot. Dip the cherries, strawberries, graham crackers and pretzels halfway into the melted chocolate. Place on the prepared baking sheets. Chill for 15 minutes or until the chocolate is set.

Yield: 40 to 50 servings

Fudge

2 cups sugar
2/3 cup evaporated milk
1/2 cup (1 stick) butter
12 marshmallows
Dash of salt
1 cup (6 ounces) semisweet
　　chocolate chips
1 cup chopped walnuts or pecans
1 teaspoon vanilla extract

Combine the sugar, evaporated milk, butter, marshmallows and salt in a saucepan. Bring to a boil over medium heat, stirring constantly. Boil for 5 minutes, stirring constantly. Remove from the heat. Add the chocolate chips, walnuts and vanilla and stir until blended. Spread immediately in a buttered 8×8-inch pan. Let stand until firm. Cut into squares.

Yield: 24 servings

Middle Tennesseans are drawn to the beach whether it be Hilton Head or somewhere along the Gulf Coast. No matter which beach, entertaining should be casual and easy.

For a great tabletop idea, fill children's plastic sand buckets with fresh or wild flowers. Scatter whole or broken shells around them or place the buckets on a large tray and sprinkle the tray with sand and shells.

Put a candle in a hurricane globe and fill with sand and small starfish or sand dollars up along the sides.

2000 - *Friends of Vanderbilt Children's Hospital donates the lead gift for the Friends Garden located at the main entrance of the new hospital.*

173

Eat Your Vegetables

chapter seven

Oven-Roasted Parmesan Asparagus

Cabbage with Bacon and Gorgonzola

Carrot Soufflé

Morris' Corn Pudding

Mother's Corn Pudding

Zesty Eggplant

Saffire's Country Green Beans

Wild Mushroom Risotto

New Potato Casserole

Sweet Potato Supreme

Gruyère Potatoes

Spinach Casserole

Acorn Squash Casserole

Squash Casserole

Tomatoes Rockefeller

Tomato and Basil Tart

Spinage Subic

Grits Soufflé

Oven-Roasted Parmesan Asparagus

FRESH CUCUMBER SALAD

Peel and thinly slice 6 to 8 large cucumbers. Place them in a large bowl and salt generously. Cover with waxed paper, place a weight on the wax paper and chill for 1 hour. Press the cucumbers and drain. Combine 1/4 cup mayonnaise, 1/3 cup sour cream, 1 tablespoon white vinegar, 1 teaspoon onion powder and 2 teaspoons sugar in a small bowl and mix well. Season with salt and pepper. Pour over the cucumbers and toss to coat. Chill, covered, for several hours. You may add 1 tablespoon chopped fresh dill, or 1/4 teaspoon cayenne pepper.

2 pounds asparagus spears, trimmed
2 tablespoons olive oil
1 tablespoon fresh lemon juice
1 teaspoon grated lemon
  zest (optional)
1 teaspoon sesame oil
Kosher salt and freshly ground
  pepper to taste
1/2 cup freshly grated
  Parmesan cheese

Photo on page 175.

Preheat the oven to 400 degrees. Place the asparagus in a roasting pan. Whisk the olive oil, lemon juice, lemon zest and sesame oil in a small bowl. Drizzle over the asparagus; toss gently to coat. Sprinkle with salt and pepper.

Bake, loosely covered, for 10 minutes. Uncover and sprinkle with the cheese. Bake, uncovered, for 5 to 10 minutes longer or just until tender; do not overcook. Serve immediately.

Note: You may substitute green beans for the asparagus.

Yield: 4 to 6 servings

2000 - The Nashville Tri Delta Alumnae Chapter celebrates the 30th anniversary of the Eve of Janus event, supporting the Pediatric Hematology/Oncology Program.

Cabbage with Bacon and Gorgonzola

6 slices bacon, chopped

3/4 cup dry white wine

1 shallot, minced

Pinch of salt

3/4 cup heavy cream

1 small head red cabbage,
    cut into halves and cut into
    1/4-inch slices

Salt and freshly ground pepper
    to taste

3/4 cup crumbled Gorgonzola cheese

1 tablespoon minced fresh parsley

Cook the bacon in a skillet over medium heat until crisp. Remove with a slotted spoon to paper towels to drain. Reserve 3 tablespoons of the drippings in the skillet; set aside.

Combine the wine, shallot and pinch of salt in a small saucepan. Bring to a boil over high heat. Reduce the heat to medium-high. Simmer until reduced to about 2 tablespoons. Stir in the cream. Simmer until reduced by half, stirring frequently.

Toss the cabbage with salt and pepper to taste in a bowl. Reheat the reserved drippings in the skillet. Add the cabbage. Sauté for 5 minutes or until the cabbage begins to wilt. Add the cream mixture. Cook for 5 to 7 minutes or until the cabbage is tender, stirring frequently. Stir in the cheese and parsley. Season with salt and pepper to taste. Cook until the cheese is melted, stirring frequently. Spoon into a serving dish. Sprinkle the cooked bacon over the top.

Yield: 4 servings

Vegetables are a great source of nutrients if they are not overcooked. Cook vegetables long enough so that they are just tender-crisp. Use a folding steamer platform that sits in most pots for steaming your vegetables.

Carrot Soufflé

2 cups mashed cooked carrots
1 cup sugar
1/2 cup (1 stick) butter, melted
3 eggs, beaten
3 tablespoons flour
1 teaspoon baking powder
1/2 teaspoon cinnamon

Preheat the oven to 400 degrees. Combine the carrots, sugar, butter, eggs, flour, baking powder and cinnamon in a bowl and mix well. Spoon into an 8×8-inch baking dish.

Bake for 15 minutes. Reduce the oven temperature to 350 degrees. Bake for 45 minutes longer.

Yield: 6 to 8 servings

Morris' Corn Pudding

1 1/2 tablespoons butter, melted
1 tablespoon flour
1 (14-ounce) can cream-style corn
1/3 cup sugar
1/3 cup milk
2 eggs, beaten
Pinch of salt
Pinch of white pepper
Pimentos for garnish

Preheat the oven to 400 degrees. Combine the butter and flour in a bowl and mix well. Add the corn, sugar, milk, eggs, salt and white pepper and mix well. Spoon into a 9-inch pie plate.

Bake for 30 to 40 minutes or until the center is set and the top and edge are starting to brown; do not overbake. Garnish with pimentos.

Yield: 8 servings

Photo on page 179.

2001 - The Children's Miracle Network Radiothon raises $105,000 *during a live three-day broadcast with partner* MIX 92.9.

Mother's Corn Pudding

When selecting vegetables for freshness, they should be brightly colored without blemishes. Beets and carrots should still have healthy greens attached. Broccoli should be free of yellow florets, and cauliflower should be tight and creamy colored. Eggplant should be medium in size and heavy, and tomatoes are best when ripened on the vine. It is best to cook vegetables until tender first when adding to a soup, as this allows for optimum flavor.

1 (14-ounce) can cream-style corn
2 eggs, beaten
1/4 cup milk
2 tablespoons flour
1 tablespoon butter, softened
1 teaspoon sugar
1/2 cup (2 ounces) shredded
    Cheddar cheese

Preheat the oven to 350 degrees. Mix the corn, eggs, milk, flour, butter and sugar in a bowl. Spoon into a greased 9×9-inch baking dish. Sprinkle the cheese over the top. Bake for 45 minutes or until set.

Yield: 6 servings

Zesty Eggplant

1 large onion, chopped
1 large red bell pepper, chopped
1/4 cup (about) extra-virgin olive oil
1 medium eggplant, or 2 small
    Italian eggplant, chopped
6 ounces mushrooms, sliced
    or chopped
1 teaspoon (about) salt
1 or 2 (14-ounce) cans diced
    tomatoes with jalapeño chiles
1 or 2 garlic cloves, chopped
Salt and pepper to taste

Sauté the onion and bell pepper in the olive oil in a skillet over medium heat just until tender and glazed. Add the eggplant and mix well. Stir in the mushrooms. Sprinkle 1 teaspoon salt over the vegetables. Cook for a few minutes, stirring constantly. Stir in the tomatoes and garlic. (For a thinner consistency, use 2 cans of tomatoes; for a thicker consistency, use 1 can.) Simmer, covered, over low heat for 30 to 40 minutes or until the vegetables are tender. Season with salt and pepper to taste. Serve hot or cold.

Yield: 4 to 6 servings

Saffire's Country Green Beans

8 ounces green beans

Salt to taste

4 ounces smoked country bacon,
    cut into small pieces

1/2 cup very thinly sliced sweet
    yellow onion

2 tablespoons sorghum

2 cups chicken stock

1 tomato, chopped

Cook the green beans in boiling salted water for about
1 minute. Remove the beans to a bowl of ice water. Let stand
until completely cool; drain and set aside.

Cook the bacon in a skillet over medium-high heat until crisp.
Add the onion. Cook until the onion is translucent, stirring
constantly. Add the green beans and sorghum and stir to coat
all the ingredients with the sorghum. Stir in the chicken stock
and tomato. Bring to a simmer. Cook for 10 to 20 minutes,
stirring occasionally.

Note: For real "country" beans, simmer the green beans for the
longer cooking time. If you like your beans more "city-style" or
crunchy, reduce the cooking time. This recipe is also delicious
with sugar snap peas or pole beans.

Yield: 4 to 6 servings

Wild Mushroom Risotto

Mushrooms are very fragile. Wipe them off with a damp cloth instead of rinsing them under the faucet since they absorb water.

2 tablespoons minced garlic

2 tablespoons olive oil

1 cup chopped yellow onion

1/2 cup chopped carrots

1 cup shiitake mushrooms, stems removed

1 cup button or cremini mushrooms

2 cups arborio rice

5 cups vegetable stock (homemade or canned)

1 1/2 cups white wine

2 tablespoons dry sherry

1/2 cup chopped seeded Roma tomatoes

2 tablespoons minced fresh Italian oregano

1 tablespoon minced fresh thyme

Salt and pepper to taste

Sauté the garlic in the olive oil in a large sauté pan for 1 minute; do not burn. Add the onion and carrots. Sauté for 1 minute. Stir in the shiitake mushrooms and button mushrooms. Sauté for 5 minutes or until the mushrooms are tender. Stir in the arborio rice. Add the vegetable stock, wine and sherry gradually, stirring until incorporated after each addition. Cook for 5 minutes, stirring frequently. (The rice will begin to release starch, which gives the risotto a creamy texture.) Stir in the tomatoes, oregano, thyme, salt and pepper. Cook until tender and creamy, stirring frequently; do not overcook. Remove from the heat. If the risotto seems a bit dry, stir in a small amount of stock just before serving.

Yield: 4 servings

New Potato Casserole

10 new potatoes, cooked and
    cut into 1/2-inch slices
3 tablespoons butter, cut into pieces
1/4 cup ranch salad dressing
2 cups (8 ounces) shredded mild or
    sharp Cheddar cheese
8 ounces bacon, crisp-cooked
    and crumbled

Preheat the oven to 350 degrees. Place the potatoes in a greased 9×13-inch baking dish. Dot with the butter. Drizzle with the salad dressing. Sprinkle with the cheese and bacon. Bake until the casserole is heated through and the cheese is melted.

Yield: 10 servings

Sweet Potato Supreme

3 cups mashed cooked
    sweet potatoes
1/2 cup granulated sugar
2 eggs, beaten
1/4 cup (1/2 stick) butter, melted
1 1/2 teaspoons vanilla extract
1/2 teaspoon salt
1 cup chopped nuts
1 cup raisins (optional)
1 cup shredded coconut (optional)
1/2 cup packed brown sugar
1/3 cup flour
1/4 cup (1/2 stick) butter, softened

Preheat the oven to 350 degrees. Combine the sweet potatoes, granulated sugar, eggs, 1/4 cup butter, vanilla and salt in a bowl and mix well. Spoon into a greased 9×13-inch baking dish.

Combine the nuts, raisins, coconut, brown sugar, flour and 1/4 cup butter in a bowl and mix well. Sprinkle over the top of the sweet potato mixture. Bake for 35 minutes or until bubbly.

Note: This dish may be prepared ahead and frozen.

Yield: 6 to 8 servings

Gruyère Potatoes

2 cups (8 ounces) shredded
    Gruyère cheese
1 to 1¹/2 cups heavy cream
¹/4 cup (¹/2 stick) unsalted
    butter, melted
1¹/2 to 2 tablespoons snipped
    fresh rosemary
1 teaspoon paprika
Kosher salt and freshly ground
    pepper to taste
2 to 3 pounds Yukon gold or red
    potatoes, thinly sliced

Photo on page 179.

Preheat the oven to 350 degrees. Combine 1 cup of the cheese, 1 cup of the cream, butter, rosemary, paprika, salt and pepper in a bowl and mix well. Layer the potatoes and cream mixture ¹/2 at a time in a greased 1¹/2-quart baking dish. Tap the baking dish gently on the countertop to evenly distribute the cream mixture.

Bake for 25 to 35 minutes. If the potatoes look dry, pour the remaining ¹/2 cup cream over the top. Sprinkle with the remaining 1 cup cheese. Bake for 10 minutes longer or until the center is bubbly and the potatoes are tender. Cool on a wire rack for about 5 minutes before serving.

Yield: 8 servings

Spinach Casserole

2 (10-ounce) packages frozen
    chopped spinach, cooked
    and well drained
1 (14-ounce) can stewed tomatoes
2 cups (8 ounces) shredded
    Cheddar cheese
1¹/2 cups cottage cheese
1 small onion, grated or chopped
2 eggs, beaten
Grated Parmesan cheese to taste
6 slices bacon, crisp-cooked
    and crumbled

Preheat the oven to 375 degrees. Squeeze the spinach to remove any excess moisture. Mix the spinach, undrained tomatoes, Cheddar cheese, cottage cheese and onion in a bowl, breaking up the tomatoes. Stir in the eggs. Spoon into a greased 9×13-inch baking dish. Sprinkle generously with Parmesan cheese; top with the bacon. Bake for 30 minutes.

Note: Recipe may be cut in half. Bake in an 8×8-inch baking dish for 15 to 20 minutes.

Yield: 8 servings

Acorn Squash Casserole

2 packages frozen winter
    squash, thawed
2 cups Coffee Rich non-dairy
    creamer
1 cup sugar
1 cup flour
3 eggs
1/4 cup (1/2 stick) butter or
    margarine, softened
Salt and pepper to taste
1 teaspoon cinnamon, or to taste

Preheat the oven to 350 degrees. Squeeze the squash to remove any excess moisture; set aside.

Beat the creamer, sugar, flour, eggs, butter, salt and pepper in a mixing bowl until well blended. Add the squash and mix well. Spoon into a buttered 9×13-inch baking dish. Bake for 30 minutes. Sprinkle with cinnamon before serving.

Yield: 12 servings

Squash Casserole

10 to 12 yellow summer squash, sliced
1 onion, chopped
1 large green bell pepper, chopped
2 tablespoons butter
1 (8-ounce) can water chestnuts,
    drained and sliced
1 cup mayonnaise
1 cup (4 ounces) shredded
    Cheddar cheese
2 eggs, lightly beaten
1 tablespoon sugar
Salt and pepper to taste
2 cups crushed cheese crackers
6 tablespoons butter or
    margarine, melted

Preheat the oven to 350 degrees. Cook the squash in boiling water until tender; drain. Mash the squash in a bowl; set aside.

Sauté the onion and bell pepper in the butter in a skillet until tender. Add the squash, water chestnuts, mayonnaise, cheese, eggs, sugar, salt and pepper and mix well. Spoon into a 9×9-inch baking dish. Combine the cheese crackers and butter in a bowl and mix well. Sprinkle over the top of the squash mixture. Bake for 1 hour.

Yield: 4 to 6 servings

Tomatoes Rockefeller

EASY MEAT LOAF

Combine 1 pound of lean ground beef, 1 package of dried onion soup mix and 2/3 cup of evaporated milk in a bowl and mix well. Shape into four small loaves and place in a shallow ungreased baking pan or dish. Pour 1 can of tomato sauce over the loaves. Bake in a preheated 350-degree oven for 30 minutes or until cooked through and brown. You may add mushrooms to the tomato sauce.

6 firm ripe tomatoes

2 (10-ounce) packages frozen
   spinach

3 eggs, beaten

1/2 cup bread crumbs

1/3 cup grated Parmesan cheese

1/4 cup (1/2 stick) butter, melted

1 tablespoon minced onion

1/2 teaspoon minced garlic

Photo on page 187.

Preheat the oven to 350 degrees. Peel and core the tomatoes and cut into halves. Drain the tomatoes cut sides down on paper towels. Arrange the tomato halves cut sides up in muffin cups or ramekins; set aside.

Cook the spinach according to the package directions; drain. Place in a strainer and press to remove any excess liquid. Combine the spinach, eggs, bread crumbs, cheese, butter, onion and garlic in a bowl and mix well. Divide among the tomato halves. Bake for 25 minutes.

Note: Tomatoes may be prepared ahead, refrigerated and baked just before serving.

Yield: 6 servings

Tomato and Basil Tart

2 cups (8 ounces) shredded
    mozzarella cheese
2 tablespoons thinly sliced
    fresh basil
1 unbaked (10-inch) pastry tart shell
4 large ripe tomatoes, thinly sliced
1/2 teaspoon salt
1/4 teaspoon pepper
1/4 cup extra-virgin olive oil

Preheat the oven to 400 degrees. Sprinkle the cheese and basil over the bottom of the tart shell. Layer with the tomato slices; sprinkle with the salt and pepper. Drizzle the olive oil over the top. Bake for 30 minutes. Serve warm or at room temperature.

Yield: 8 servings

Spinage Subic

4 cups chopped fresh spinach, or
    1 small bag frozen chopped
    spinach, thawed
1/4 cup chicken broth
2 cups fresh green peas, or 1 small
    bag frozen peas
1/2 cup chicken broth
2 shallots, minced and sautéed
1/8 teaspoon salt
1/8 teaspoon white pepper
1/8 teaspoon freshly ground nutmeg
1 egg white, beaten

Preheat the oven to 350 degrees. Cook the spinach in 1/4 cup chicken broth in a saucepan for 5 minutes or until tender; set aside.

Cook the peas in 1/2 cup chicken broth in a saucepan for 8 to 10 minutes or until tender. Purée the peas with the broth in a blender. Fold into the spinach. Add the shallots, salt, pepper and nutmeg and mix well. Fold in the egg white. Spoon into a greased 1-quart baking dish. Bake for 20 to 30 minutes or until set.

Yield: 4 servings

Grits Soufflé

3 cups water

1 teaspoon kosher salt

2 cups yellow grits

3 cups milk

$1/2$ cup (1 stick) unsalted butter

1 tablespoon sugar

2 cups (8 ounces) shredded
    pepper-Jack cheese

1 cup yellow corn kernels
    (2 ears of corn)

4 eggs, lightly beaten

1 red bell pepper, chopped

1 jalapeño chile, seeded
    and chopped

1 tablespoon thyme

2 teaspoons kosher salt

$1/2$ teaspoon freshly ground pepper

Preheat the oven to 350 degrees. Combine the water and 1 teaspoon of the salt in a saucepan. Bring to a boil. Reduce the heat to medium. Add the grits in a steady stream, whisking constantly. Cook for 10 minutes or until thickened, stirring constantly. Add $1^{1}/2$ cups of the milk. Cook for 3 to 5 minutes or until the milk is absorbed, stirring constantly. Remove from the heat. Add the remaining $1^{1}/2$ cups milk, butter and sugar and mix well. Stir in the cheese, corn, eggs, bell pepper, jalapeño chile, thyme, 2 teaspoons salt and pepper and mix well.

Pour into a buttered 4-quart soufflé dish. Bake for 45 to 55 minutes or until the soufflé has risen and is set around the edge; the center should be slightly soft. Let stand for 5 minutes. Serve warm.

Yield: 8 servings

Sweet Endings

chapter eight

Raspberry Mousse

Chocolate Mousse

Burnt Cream

The Perfect Blackberry Cobbler

Homemade Milky Way Ice Cream

Tish's Mocha Cream Dessert

Bread Pudding with Whiskey Sauce

Mario's Tiramisu

The Yellow Porch Chocolate Torte

Strawberry Cake

Chocolate Molten Cakes with Raspberry Coulis

Italian Cream Cake

Nona's Chocolate Cake

Carrot Cake

Chocolate Sour Cream Pound Cake

Cream Cheese Pound Cake

Coconut Pound Cake

Coconut Cake with White Glossy Icing

Tennessee Jam Cake with Penuche Frosting

Frozen Peppermint Cheesecake

Cheesecake

Blueberry-Topped Cheesecake Bars

Apple Apple Pie

Big Frances' Chocolate Chess Pie

Coconut Cream Pie

Coffee Toffee Pie

Fudge Pie with Raspberry Coulis

Gooey Fudge Pie

Congressional Cherry Pie

Creamy Cheesecake Pie

Peach Crumble Pie

Lemon Icebox Pie

Margarita Mud Pie

Lamar Alexander's Peanut Butter Silk Pie

Music City Pumpkin Pie

Chocolate Éclairs and Cream Puffs

Abby's Toffee Blondies

The Best Lemon Bars

Crescent Cookies

French Lace Cookies

Lace Oatmeal Cookies

Lindzer Tarts

Raspberry Mousse

2 (12-ounce) packages frozen
   sweetened raspberries, thawed
1 envelope unflavored gelatin
3 tablespoons cold water
1¹/2 cups whipping cream
¹/2 cup confectioners' sugar, sifted
Light corn syrup
Granulated sugar

Purée the raspberries in a food processor. Strain through a sieve into a bowl, pressing to remove the seeds. Reserve 2 cups of the raspberry purée in the bowl, saving the remaining purée for another use.

Soften the gelatin in the cold water in a bowl. Place over simmering water for about 30 seconds or until the gelatin is completely dissolved, whisking constantly. Whisk into the raspberry purée, working quickly to prevent the gelatin from forming strands.

Beat the cream with the confectioners' sugar in a mixing bowl until soft peaks form. Fold into the raspberry mixture.

Dip the rims of 8 individual dessert dishes into corn syrup, tapping gently to remove any excess. Dip immediately into granulated sugar to coat. Spoon the raspberry mousse into the prepared dishes. Chill, covered, until serving time.

Photo on page 191.

Yield: 8 servings

Chocolate Mousse

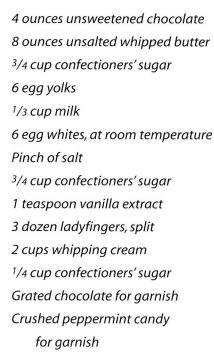

4 ounces unsweetened chocolate

8 ounces unsalted whipped butter

3/4 cup confectioners' sugar

6 egg yolks

1/3 cup milk

6 egg whites, at room temperature

Pinch of salt

3/4 cup confectioners' sugar

1 teaspoon vanilla extract

3 dozen ladyfingers, split

2 cups whipping cream

1/4 cup confectioners' sugar

Grated chocolate for garnish

Crushed peppermint candy
    for garnish

Melt the chocolate in a double boiler over simmering water. Cream the butter and 3/4 cup confectioners' sugar in a mixing bowl. Add the egg yolks and milk and mix well. Stir into the melted chocolate. Cook until thickened. Remove from the heat. Let stand until cool.

Beat the egg whites with salt in a large mixing bowl until stiff peaks form. Beat in 3/4 cup confectioners' sugar. Fold in the chocolate mixture and vanilla.

Line the bottom and side of a deep serving dish with 1/3 of the ladyfingers. Layer the chocolate mousse and remaining ladyfingers 1/2 at a time in the dish. Chill, covered, for 8 to 12 hours.

Beat the cream with 1/4 cup confectioners' sugar in a mixing bowl until stiff peaks form. Spread carefully over the chocolate mousse. Sprinkle with grated chocolate and crushed peppermint candy.

Yield: 10 to 12 servings

If you are in the middle of a recipe and find you are all out of chocolate squares, simply use cocoa and shortening. One square of chocolate equals three tablespoons cocoa and one tablespoon shortening. Now you're back in chocolate paradise!

Burnt Cream

2 cups heavy cream

4 egg yolks

1/2 cup sugar

1 tablespoon vanilla extract

1/4 cup sugar

Preheat the oven to 350 degrees. Heat the cream in a saucepan over low heat until bubbles form around the edge of the pan. Beat the egg yolks and 1/2 cup sugar in a mixing bowl for 3 minutes or until thickened. Add the cream gradually, whisking constantly. Stir in the vanilla. Pour into six 6-ounce custard cups or blini pans. Place the custard cups in a baking pan. Pour enough warm water into the baking pan to reach halfway up the sides of the custard cups.

Bake for 30 to 45 minutes or until set. Remove the custard cups from the pan. Refrigerate, covered, until well chilled.

Preheat the broiler. Sprinkle 2 teaspoons sugar on the top of each custard. Place on a baking sheet. Broil until the sugar has caramelized. Chill, covered, until serving time.

Note: Garnish with fresh raspberries for a dramatic presentation.

Photo on page 195.

Yield: 6 servings

The Perfect Blackberry Cobbler

Is your ice cream burning? Freezer burning that is. . .to keep that from happening, when the ice cream is a bit softened, place plastic wrap directly on top, touching the entire surface. This prevents air from burning the top, and your ice cream will stay perfect for days.

FILLING

1 1/2 cups water

1 cup sugar

1/2 cup water

1/4 cup cornstarch

6 cups fresh blackberries
    or frozen blackberries,
    partially thawed

1/4 cup (1/2 stick) butter,
    cut into pieces

CRUST

1 cup sifted flour

1/2 teaspoon salt

2 tablespoons cold milk

1/4 cup vegetable oil

1 tablespoon butter, melted

1 tablespoon sugar

Vanilla ice cream

Preheat the oven to 375 degrees. For the filling, combine 1 1/2 cups of the water and sugar in a saucepan. Bring to a boil, stirring frequently. Combine the remaining 1/2 cup water and cornstarch in a small bowl and mix well. Stir into the sugar mixture. Return to a boil, stirring constantly. Reduce the heat. Simmer for 1 minute or until thickened, stirring frequently. Remove from the heat. Add the blackberries and butter and stir until the butter is melted. Pour into a 9×9-inch baking pan.

For the crust, mix the flour and salt in a medium bowl. Add the milk and oil and stir until a dough forms. Shape into a ball. Place on a lightly floured surface. Roll into a square large enough to fit into the baking pan. Place the dough over the filling. Brush with the butter and sprinkle with the sugar.

Bake for 40 minutes or until the crust is browned and the filling is bubbly. Cool on a wire rack. Serve warm with vanilla ice cream.

Yield: 6 servings

 *The Monroe Carell Jr. Children's Hospital at Vanderbilt opened February 8 after five years of construction. The eight-floor, 616,785 square foot facility is the largest building on the Vanderbilt Campus.*

Homemade Milky Way Ice Cream

12 (2-ounce) Milky Way candy
    bars, chopped
1 (14-ounce) can sweetened
    condensed milk
3/4 cup chocolate syrup
Milk

Melt the candy bars in a double boiler over simmering water. Add the sweetened condensed milk and chocolate syrup and beat until smooth. Pour into an ice cream freezer container; add enough milk to reach the fill line. Freeze according to the manufacturer's directions.

Yield: 1 to 1 1/2 gallons

Tish's Mocha Cream Dessert

1 tablespoon instant coffee granules
1 cup boiling water
30 large marshmallows
1 cup heavy cream
1 teaspoon vanilla extract
Whipped cream for garnish
Crushed English toffee candy bars
    for garnish

Dissolve the instant coffee granules in the boiling water in a bowl. Add the marshmallows and stir until melted. Stir in 1 cup cream. Let stand until cool. Stir in the vanilla. Chill, covered, for 3 hours. Top with whipped cream and crushed toffee candy bars.

Note: This dessert is beautiful served in individual ramekins or a crystal bowl.

Yield: 3 to 4 servings

The hospital collaborates with six other children's hospitals to develop the Pediatric Advanced
2004 - *Comfort Team (PACT), a group of doctors, nurses, counselors, clergy, and parents who help families cope with a child's terminal illness.*

197

Bread Pudding with Whiskey Sauce

3/4 cup raisins

Bourbon

1 (1-pound) loaf French bread,
    torn into small pieces

2 cups heavy cream

2 cups milk

1/3 cup butter, melted

2 cups sugar

3 eggs

1 tablespoon vanilla extract

1 1/2 teaspoons ground cinnamon

1 teaspoon apple pie spice

3/4 cup chopped pecans

Cinnamon for sprinkling

Whiskey Sauce (below)

Combine the raisins and enough bourbon to cover in a bowl. Let stand, covered, for 8 to 12 hours.

Preheat the oven to 350 degrees. Combine the bread, cream, milk and butter in a bowl. Let stand for 10 minutes.

Combine the sugar, eggs, vanilla, 1 1/2 teaspoons cinnamon and apple pie spice in a bowl and mix well. Pour over the bread mixture. Stir in the pecans and raisins. Spoon into a greased 9×13-inch baking pan. Sprinkle with cinnamon.

Bake for 1 hour or until the pudding is set. Spoon into individual dessert dishes; top with Whiskey Sauce.

Yield: 12 servings

Whiskey Sauce

1 cup sugar

1 cup half-and-half

1/2 cup (1 stick) butter

1/4 cup cold water

2 tablespoons cornstarch

3/4 cup bourbon, or to taste

Combine the sugar, half-and-half and butter in a heavy saucepan. Cook over medium heat until the sugar is dissolved and the butter is melted, stirring frequently. Combine the water and cornstarch in a bowl and mix well. Sir into the sugar mixture. Bring to a boil. Cook for 1 minute, stirring constantly. Remove from the heat. Stir in the bourbon.

2004 - *Friends of Vanderbilt Children's Hospital gives lead gift to purchase a pediatric ambulance.*

Mario's Tiramisu

1¾ cups hot black coffee

¼ cup sugar

10½ ounces bittersweet chocolate

1¾ cups mascarpone
    cheese, softened

⅔ cup whipping cream, whipped
    to soft peaks

6 tablespoons dark rum or brandy

36 ladyfingers

Baking cocoa for dusting

Combine the hot coffee and sugar in a bowl and mix well. Let stand until cool. Melt the chocolate in a heatproof bowl over a saucepan of simmering water, stirring occasionally. Remove from the heat. Cool slightly.

Beat the mascarpone cheese in a mixing bowl until fluffy. Fold in the whipped cream. Stir in the chocolate; set aside.

Add the rum to the coffee mixture and mix well. Dip the ladyfingers briefly into the coffee mixture just until moistened but not soggy. Place 3 ladyfingers on each of 4 serving plates. Spoon ½ of the chocolate mixture over the ladyfingers, dividing evenly. Repeat the layers of ladyfingers and chocolate mixture. Top with the remaining ladyfingers. Chill, covered, for at least 1 hour. Dust a small amount of baking cocoa over the top just before serving.

Note: For a pretty presentation, serve the tiramisu in a trifle dish or Champagne glasses or goblets.

Yield: 4 servings

The Yellow Porch Chocolate Torte

2 cups (4 sticks) butter
8 ounces brown sugar
    (about 1 cup packed)
1 cup strong brewed coffee
2 teaspoons vanilla extract
1 pound semisweet chocolate chips
    (about 2²/3 cups)
8 eggs, beaten

Preheat the oven to 350 degrees. Combine the butter, brown sugar, coffee and vanilla in a saucepan and mix well. Bring to a simmer, stirring frequently. Remove from the heat. Add the chocolate chips and stir until melted. Stir a small amount of the chocolate mixture into the beaten eggs; stir the eggs into the chocolate mixture. Pour into a parchment or waxed paper-lined 9-inch springform pan. Wrap the outside of the pan with foil. Place in a large baking pan. Add water to the large pan to a depth of 1/2 inch. Bake for 1 hour or until the torte jiggles like a custard. Remove from the water bath. Let stand to cool on a wire rack. Chill, covered, for 8 to 12 hours to let the torte settle and become dense.

Remove the side of the pan. Invert onto a serving plate. Remove the bottom of the pan and the parchment paper.

Note: Use good-quality chocolate chips for the best results. You may substitute bittersweet chocolate chips for part of the semisweet chocolate chips for a richer torte.

Yield: 12 servings

2004 - *Friends of Vanderbilt Children's Hospital forms a regional board of directors.*

Strawberry Cake

1 (2-layer) package butter-flavor
   cake mix
2/3 cup buttermilk
1/2 cup (1 stick) butter, softened
2 eggs
1/2 cup strawberry preserves
2 cups whipping cream
2 tablespoons confectioners' sugar
2 quarts strawberries, sliced

Preheat the oven to 350 degrees. Beat the cake mix, buttermilk, butter and eggs at low speed in a mixing bowl until the cake mix is moistened. Beat at medium speed for 4 minutes. Pour into 2 greased and floured 9-inch round cake pans. Bake for 18 to 20 minutes or until a wooden pick inserted into the center of the layers comes out clean. Cool in the pans for 10 minutes. Remove to wire racks. Brush the top of each layer with 2 tablespoons of the preserves. Cool completely.

Beat the whipping cream, remaining 1/4 cup preserves and confectioners' sugar at high speed in a mixing bowl until stiff peaks form. Place 1 cake layer on a serving plate. Arrange 1/2 of the strawberries on top; spread with 1/2 of the whipped cream mixture. Top with the remaining cake layer, strawberries and whipped cream mixture.

Yield: 10 to 12 servings

Chocolate Molten Cakes with Raspberry Coulis

RASPBERRY COULIS

2 1/2 cups fresh raspberries or frozen
    raspberries, thawed
1 tablespoon confectioners' sugar
1 tablespoon fresh lemon juice

CAKES

6 ounces good-quality bittersweet
    chocolate, chopped
10 tablespoons unsalted butter,
    cut into pieces
3 eggs
3 egg yolks
1 1/2 cups confectioners' sugar
1/2 cup flour
1 tablespoon vanilla extract

Vanilla bean ice cream

For the raspberry coulis, purée the raspberries in a blender or food processor. Strain through a sieve into a bowl to remove the seeds. Stir in the confectioners' sugar and lemon juice. Chill, covered, until ready to use. (May be prepared up to 1 day in advance.)

For the cakes, preheat the oven to 450 degrees. Butter 8 large muffin cups or ramekins generously and dust lightly with baking cocoa. Melt the chocolate and butter in a heavy saucepan over low heat, stirring constantly. Remove from the heat. Cool slightly.

Whisk the eggs and egg yolks in a small bowl. Add the chocolate mixture, confectioners' sugar, flour and vanilla and mix well. Divide among the prepared muffin cups. Bake for 11 minutes or just until the centers look barely set. (The inside should remain liquid.) Run a small knife around the edges of the muffin cups to loosen the cakes. Remove to dessert plates. Serve immediately with the raspberry coulis and ice cream.

Photo on page 202.

Yield: 8 servings

RECIPE FOR HAPPINESS

Combine 2 heaping cups of patience, 1 heart full of love, 2 handfuls of generosity, a dash of laughter and 1 head full of understanding. Sprinkle generously with kindness. Add plenty of faith and mix well. Spread over a period of a lifetime. Serve to everyone you meet.

Italian Cream Cake

1/2 cup (1 stick) margarine, softened

1/2 cup vegetable oil

2 cups sugar

5 egg yolks

1 teaspoon baking soda

2 cups flour

1 cup buttermilk

1 cup chopped English walnuts

1 (3-ounce) can flaked coconut

1 teaspoon vanilla extract

5 egg whites, stiffly beaten

Cream Cheese Frosting (below)

Preheat the oven to 350 degrees. Cream the margarine and oil in a mixing bowl until light and fluffy. Add the sugar and egg yolks and mix well. Combine the baking soda and flour and mix well. Add to the creamed mixture alternately with the buttermilk, mixing well after each addition. Stir in the walnuts, coconut and vanilla. Fold in the egg whites. Pour into 3 greased 9-inch round cake pans. Bake for 25 minutes or until the layers test done. Cool in the pans for 10 minutes. Remove to wire racks to cool completely. Spread the Cream Cheese Frosting between the layers and over the top and side of the cake.

Yield: 15 to 20 servings

Cream Cheese Frosting

8 ounces cream cheese, softened

1/2 cup (1 stick) margarine, softened

1 (1-pound) package
   confectioners' sugar

1 teaspoon vanilla extract

1/2 cup chopped English walnuts

Cream the cream cheese and margarine in a mixing bowl until light and fluffy. Beat in the confectioners' sugar and vanilla until smooth. Stir in the walnuts.

Cheesecake

16 ounces cream cheese, softened

1 cup sugar

2 tablespoons flour

1 teaspoon vanilla extract

1/2 teaspoon salt

1/2 teaspoon almond extract

4 egg yolks

1 cup heavy cream

4 egg whites, stiffly beaten

1 (9-inch) graham cracker pie shell

1 quart strawberries, sliced

3 tablespoons sugar

2 tablespoons lemon juice

1 tablespoon cornstarch

Preheat the oven to 325 degrees. Beat the cream cheese, 1 cup sugar, flour, vanilla, salt and almond extract in a large mixing bowl until mixed. Add the egg yolks, beating just until mixed. Stir in the cream. Fold in the beaten egg whites. Pour into the pie shell. Bake for 1 hour or until set. Cool completely on a wire rack. Refrigerate, covered, until chilled.

Combine the strawberries, 3 tablespoons sugar, lemon juice and cornstarch in a saucepan and mix well. Cook until of glaze consistency, stirring constantly; cool. Pour over the top of the cheesecake. Chill, covered, until ready to serve.

Note: You may prepare your own graham cracker crust using the recipe on the package of graham cracker crumbs and adding 1 cup chopped pecans.

Yield: 6 to 8 servings

Nona's Chocolate Cake

2 cups sifted flour
2 cups sugar
1 cup (2 sticks) margarine
1 cup water
1/4 cup baking cocoa
1/2 cup buttermilk
2 eggs
1 teaspoon baking soda
1 teaspoon vanilla extract
Chocolate Icing (below)

Preheat the oven to 350 degrees. Combine the flour and sugar in a bowl and mix well; set aside. Combine the margarine, water and baking cocoa in a saucepan. Bring to a boil, stirring constantly. Pour over the flour mixture and mix well. Add the buttermilk, eggs, baking soda and vanilla and mix well. Pour into a greased and floured 10×15-inch cake pan. Bake for 25 minutes or until the cake tests done. Pour the Chocolate Icing over the hot cake immediately.

Yield: 8 to 10 servings

Eggs should be used in recipes at room temperature as this allows for great texture and volume. Eggs are perfect for thickening a sauce because egg yolks are nearly 1/3 fat. In desserts, when beating egg whites, confectioners' sugar will reduce whipped egg white volume. Whipped to stiffest point is when you tip the bowl and the egg whites do not slide out.

Chocolate Icing

1/2 cup (1 stick) margarine
   or butter
1/4 cup baking cocoa
4 to 6 tablespoons milk
1 (1-pound) package
   confectioners' sugar

Combine the margarine, baking cocoa and milk in a saucepan. Bring to a boil. Place the confectioners' sugar in a bowl and add the margarine mixture. Whisk until well blended.

Carrot Cake

2 cups flour

2 cups sugar

1 teaspoon baking powder

1 teaspoon baking soda

1 teaspoon salt

1 teaspoon ground cinnamon

3 cups finely shredded baby carrots

1 cup vegetable oil

4 eggs

Cream Cheese Frosting (below)

Preheat the oven to 325 degrees. Combine the flour, sugar, baking powder, baking soda, salt and cinnamon in a mixing bowl and mix well. Add the carrots, oil and eggs. Beat at low speed until the dry ingredients are moistened. Beat at medium speed for 2 minutes. Pour into 2 greased and lightly floured 9-inch round cake pans. Bake for 40 minutes or until the layers test done. Cool in the pans for 10 minutes. Remove to wire racks to cool completely. Spread the Cream Cheese Frosting between the layers and over the top and side of the cake.

Note: For a 9×13-inch cake, increase the baking time to 50 to 60 minutes. Be sure to use baby carrots for a moist, flavorful cake.

Photo on page 206.

Yield: 8 to 10 servings

Cream Cheese Frosting

6 ounces cream cheese, softened

1/2 cup (1 stick) butter or
   margarine, softened

2 tablespoons vanilla extract

4 cups sifted confectioners' sugar

Beat the cream cheese, butter and vanilla in a mixing bowl until light and fluffy. Add the confectioners' sugar gradually, beating until smooth.

Chocolate Sour Cream Pound Cake

2 cups flour

¹/₂ cup baking cocoa

1 teaspoon baking powder

¹/₂ teaspoon salt

1 cup (2 sticks) unsalted butter,
    slightly softened

2 cups granulated sugar

1 cup packed dark brown sugar

5 eggs, at room temperature,
    lightly beaten

1 cup sour cream

1 teaspoon vanilla extract

¹/₂ teaspoon almond extract

Preheat the oven to 325 degrees. Sift the flour, baking cocoa, baking powder and salt together; set aside. Cream the butter in a mixing bowl until light and fluffy. Add the granulated sugar gradually, beating constantly. Add the brown sugar and beat just until fluffy; scrape down the side of the bowl. Add the eggs in a slow, steady stream, beating constantly. Add the sour cream, vanilla extract and almond extract and mix well. Beat in the flour mixture at low speed until almost blended. Finish blending with a rubber spatula, folding until the batter is smooth and well mixed, scraping the bottom and side of the bowl. Pour into a greased and floured 10- to 12-cup bundt pan.

Bake for 50 to 75 minutes or until the cake is set and a wooden pick inserted into the center of the cake comes out with a few clinging crumbs. Cool in the pan for 8 minutes or until the cake pulls away from the side of the pan. Invert onto a wire rack. Cool completely before serving.

Yield: 16 servings

Cream Cheese Pound Cake

1¹/₂ cups (3 sticks) unsalted
   butter, softened
8 ounces cream cheese, softened
3 cups sugar
6 eggs, at room temperature
3 cups flour
1 teaspoon salt
¹/₄ cup buttermilk
2 teaspoons vanilla extract
1 teaspoon almond extract

Preheat the oven to 325 degrees. Grease and flour a 10-inch tube pan and line the bottom with parchment paper. Cream the butter and cream cheese in a mixing bowl until smooth. Add the sugar gradually, beating until fluffy. Add the eggs 1 at a time, beating well after each addition. Add the flour, salt, buttermilk, vanilla extract and almond extract and mix just until moistened. Pour into the prepared pan. Bake for 1 hour and 20 minutes or until a wooden pick inserted into the center of the cake comes out clean. Cool in the pan for 10 minutes. Invert onto a serving plate.

Yield: 10 to 12 servings

Coconut Pound Cake

1 cup vegetable oil
¹/₂ cup (1 stick) butter, softened
6 egg yolks, at room temperature
3 cups sugar
¹/₂ teaspoon almond extract
¹/₂ teaspoon coconut extract
3 cups flour, sifted
1 cup milk
7 ounces shredded coconut
6 egg whites, at room temperature

Preheat the oven to 300 degrees. Beat the oil, butter and egg yolks at high speed in a mixing bowl until well blended. Add the sugar gradually, beating until light and fluffy. Beat in the almond extract and coconut extract. Add the flour and milk alternately, mixing well at low speed after each addition. Fold in the coconut. Beat the egg whites in a mixing bowl until stiff peaks form. Fold gently into the batter. Pour into a greased and floured 10-inch bundt pan. Bake for 1¹/₂ hours or just until the cake tests done; do not overbake. Cool in the pan for 10 minutes. Invert onto a serving plate.

Note: This very moist, dense cake freezes well.

Yield: 10 to 12 servings

Coconut Cake with White Glossy Icing

3/4 cup shortening

1 1/2 cups sugar

3 egg yolks

1/2 teaspoon coconut extract

2 1/4 cups cake flour

2 teaspoons baking powder

1/2 teaspoon salt

1 cup milk

1 cup flaked coconut

3 egg whites

White Glossy Icing (below)

2 cups flaked coconut

Preheat the oven to 350 degrees. Cream the shortening in a mixing bowl. Add the sugar gradually, beating until light and fluffy. Add the egg yolks 1 at a time, beating well after each addition. Stir in the coconut extract. Sift the cake flour, baking powder and salt together. Add to the creamed mixture alternately with the milk, beating well after each addition. Stir in 1 cup coconut. Beat the egg whites in a mixing bowl until stiff moist peaks form. Stir 1/3 of the beaten egg whites into the batter. Fold in the remaining egg whites gently. Pour into a buttered and lightly floured 9×13-inch cake pan.

Bake for 25 minutes or until a wooden pick inserted into the center comes out clean. Cool in the pan for 20 minutes. Spread the White Glossy Icing over the cooled cake. Sprinkle 2 cups coconut over the top. Chill, covered, until serving time.

Yield: 10 to 12 servings

White Glossy Icing

1 1/2 cups sugar

2 egg whites

1/4 cup water

1/4 teaspoon cream of tartar

1/8 teaspoon salt

1/2 cup shredded coconut

Combine the sugar, egg whites, water, cream of tartar and salt in a heatproof bowl and mix well. Place over simmering water. Beat over low heat for 5 to 7 minutes or until the icing forms peaks. Remove from the heat. Continue beating until the icing thickens to a spreadable consistency. Fold in the coconut gently.

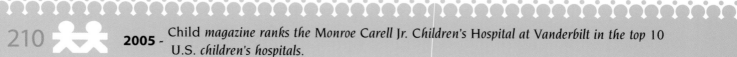

Tennessee Jam Cake with Penuche Frosting

1 cup margarine, softened
1 1/2 cups sugar
1 cup seedless blackberry jam
4 eggs
2 1/2 cups flour
1 teaspoon baking soda
1 teaspoon grated nutmeg
1 teaspoon ground cinnamon
1 teaspoon ground cloves
1/4 teaspoon salt
1 cup buttermilk
1 1/2 cups chopped pecans
Penuche Frosting (below)

Preheat the oven to 350 degrees. Cream the margarine and sugar in a mixing bowl until light and fluffy. Add the blackberry jam and eggs and mix well. Sift the flour, baking soda, nutmeg, cinnamon, cloves and salt together. Add to the creamed mixture alternately with the buttermilk, mixing well after each addition. Fold in the pecans. Pour into 3 greased 9-inch round cake pans.

Bake for 30 to 35 minutes or until the layers test done. Cool in the pans for 10 minutes. Remove to wire racks to cool completely. Spread the Penuche Frosting between the layers and over the top and side of the cooled cake.

Yield: 10 to 12 servings

Penuche Frosting

1 1/2 cups packed dark brown sugar
3/4 cup granulated sugar
1/2 cup milk
3 tablespoons butter
1 1/2 tablespoons corn syrup
1/8 teaspoon salt
1 1/2 teaspoons vanilla extract

Combine the brown sugar, granulated sugar, milk, butter, corn syrup and salt in a heavy saucepan. Bring to a boil over low heat, stirring constantly. Boil for 1 minute. Remove from the heat. Let cool to lukewarm. Add the vanilla and beat until thick enough to spread.

Frozen Peppermint Cheesecake

CRUST

1 1/2 cups chocolate wafer crumbs

1/4 cup sugar

1/4 cup (1/2 stick) butter, melted

FILLING

8 ounces cream cheese, softened

1 (14-ounce) can sweetened
    condensed milk

1 cup crushed hard
    peppermint candy

3 drops of red food coloring

2 cups whipping cream, whipped

Whipped cream for garnish

Whole and crushed hard
    peppermint candy for garnish

Hot Chocolate Sauce (below)

Photo on page 213.

For the crust, combine the wafer crumbs, sugar and butter in a bowl and mix well. Press over the bottom and 1 inch up the side of a 9-inch springform pan. Refrigerate until chilled.

For the filling, beat the cream cheese at high speed in a mixing bowl until fluffy. Add the sweetened condensed milk, 1 cup crushed peppermint candy and food coloring and mix well. Fold in 2 cups whipped cream. Pour into the chilled crust. Freeze, covered, until set. Garnish with whipped cream and peppermint candy. Drizzle with Hot Chocolate Sauce.

Note: You may double the crust ingredients if you want the crust to come all the way up the side of the cheesecake.

Yield: 10 to 12 servings

Hot Chocolate Sauce

1 cup (6 ounces) semisweet
    chocolate chips

1/2 cup (1 stick) butter

2 cups confectioners' sugar

1 (12-ounce) can evaporated milk

1 teaspoon vanilla extract

Melt the chocolate chips and butter in a saucepan over low heat, stirring frequently. Add the confectioners' sugar and evaporated milk and mix well. Cook for 8 minutes or until thickened, stirring frequently. Stir in the vanilla.

Blueberry-Topped Cheesecake Bars

CRUST

1 cup flour

1 cup finely chopped pecans

¹/₂ cup (1 stick) butter, melted

¹/₄ cup packed light brown sugar

FILLING

16 ounces cream cheese, softened

1 cup sugar

1 teaspoon vanilla extract

2 eggs

SOUR CREAM TOPPING

2 cups sour cream

¹/₃ cup sugar

1 teaspoon vanilla extract

BLUEBERRY TOPPING

¹/₄ cup water

1¹/₂ teaspoons cornstarch

²/₃ cup sugar

3 tablespoons honey

1 (12-ounce) package frozen
    blueberries, partially thawed, or
    3 cups fresh blueberries

For the crust, preheat the oven to 350 degrees. Line a 9×13-inch baking pan with foil; grease the foil lightly. Combine the flour, pecans, butter and brown sugar in a bowl and mix well. Press over the bottom of the prepared pan. Bake for 10 to 15 minutes or until lightly browned.

For the filling, beat the cream cheese, sugar and vanilla in a mixing bowl until blended. Add the eggs and beat well. Spread over the crust. Bake for 20 minutes.

For the sour cream topping, combine the sour cream, sugar and vanilla in a bowl and mix well. Pour over the filling. Bake for 3 to 5 minutes; cool. Refrigerate, covered, until chilled.

For the blueberry topping, whisk the water and cornstarch in a heavy saucepan until blended. Stir in the sugar and honey. Bring to a boil over medium-high heat, stirring constantly. Add the blueberries. Bring to a boil. Cook for 5 minutes or just until the berries burst but still maintain their shape, gently stirring occasionally. Remove from the heat. Cool completely. (Mixture thickens as it cools.) Spread over the chilled sour cream topping. Cut into 1-inch squares.

Note: To easily cut into squares, place the pan of cooled cheesecake in the freezer for 1 hour. Spread with the blueberry topping; freeze again. When ready to cut, remove the foil liner and cut into squares. Return the cut cheesecake to the freezer until ready to serve.

Yield: 24 servings

Apple Apple Pie

1 1/2 cups sugar

2 teaspoons ground cinnamon

1/4 teaspoon salt

1/2 cup (1 stick) butter, melted

3 cups chopped Ambrosia apples, or
    other sweet apples

1 egg, beaten

1 (2-crust) pie pastry

Preheat the oven to 400 degrees. Combine the sugar, cinnamon and salt in a bowl and mix well. Add the butter and mix well. Stir in the apples and egg. Fit half the pastry into a pie plate. Spoon in the apple filling. Top with the remaining pastry, fluting the edge and cutting vents. Bake for 10 minutes. Reduce the oven temperature to 350 degrees. Bake for 40 minutes longer.

Yield: 6 to 8 servings

Big Frances' Chocolate Chess Pie

3 1/2 cups sugar

6 tablespoons baking cocoa

2 tablespoons butter, melted

6 eggs

1 (12-ounce) can evaporated milk

1 tablespoon vanilla extract

3 baked (9-inch) piecrusts

Preheat the oven to 350 degrees. Combine the sugar, baking cocoa and butter in a bowl and mix well. Whisk in the eggs. Add the evaporated milk and vanilla and mix well. Divide evenly among the piecrusts. Bake for 35 minutes or until a knife inserted into the centers comes out clean.

Yield: 18 to 24 servings

Coconut Cream Pie

1/4 cup sugar

3 tablespoons cornstarch

1/4 teaspoon salt

2 cups scalded milk

1 tablespoon butter

2 egg yolks, beaten

1/2 cup shredded coconut

1 teaspoon vanilla extract

1 baked (9-inch) piecrust

2 egg whites

1/4 teaspoon cream of tartar

2 tablespoons sugar

1/4 cup shredded coconut

Preheat the oven to 350 degrees. Combine 1/4 cup sugar, cornstarch and salt in a double boiler. Add the milk gradually, stirring constantly. Add the butter. Cook over boiling water until thickened, stirring constantly. Stir a small amount of the hot mixture into the beaten egg yolks; stir the egg yolks into the hot mixture. Cook until thickened, stirring constantly. Remove from the heat. Cool slightly. Stir in 1/2 cup coconut and vanilla. Pour into the piecrust.

Beat the egg whites with the cream of tartar in a mixing bowl until soft peaks form. Add 2 tablespoons sugar gradually, beating until stiff peaks form. Spread over the top of the pie. Sprinkle with 1/4 cup coconut. Bake for 10 minutes or until the meringue is browned.

Note: If raw eggs are a problem in your area, use meringue powder and follow the package instructions.

Yield: 6 to 8 servings

Always use natural fibers for your napkins and placemats. Use 100 percent cotton for more informal breakfasts and lunches and damask or linen for formal dinners. Never use synthetic or polyester materials. They do not absorb well.

Coffee Toffee Pie

CRUST

1/4 cup sugar

1 1/2 cups crisp rice cereal, partially
   crushed

1/2 ounce good-quality bittersweet
   chocolate, finely chopped
   (about 1 1/2 tablespoons)

FILLING

2 teaspoons instant coffee granules

2 cups low-fat milk

1/2 teaspoon unflavored gelatin

3 tablespoons cornstarch

3 ounces good-quality bittersweet
   chocolate, finely chopped

1/4 cup packed light brown sugar

2 teaspoons dark rum

TOPPING

1/3 cup whipping cream, well chilled

1 teaspoon light brown sugar

1/4 teaspoon instant coffee granules

1 teaspoon dark rum

Bittersweet chocolate shavings
   for garnish

For the crust, place the sugar in a small nonstick skillet. Cook over medium heat until starting to melt; do not stir. Continue cooking for 2 to 3 minutes or until the sugar is melted and turns a deep golden caramel color, stirring occasionally with a fork. Remove from the heat. Stir in the cereal. Remove immediately to an 8- or 9-inch pie plate, pressing evenly over the bottom and slightly up the side. Sprinkle with the chocolate; let stand until melted. Spread the melted chocolate evenly over the crust with the back of a spoon. Cool until the chocolate is set.

For the filling, dissolve the instant coffee in 2 tablespoons of the milk in a small bowl. Stir in the gelatin; let stand until softened. Whisk the cornstarch and remaining 1 7/8 cups milk in a heavy 2-quart saucepan. Bring to a simmer over low heat, stirring constantly. (This will take about 15 minutes; low-fat milk curdles easily if heated too quickly.) Continue simmering for 2 minutes, stirring constantly. Remove from the heat. Add the gelatin mixture, chocolate, brown sugar and rum. Whisk for 1 minute or until smooth and the gelatin is completely dissolved. Remove to a metal bowl placed in a large bowl of ice water. Cool the filling for 3 to 5 minutes or until room temperature, whisking constantly to ensure the gelatin sets evenly. Pour into the crust. Chill, covered, for 3 hours or until set.

For the topping, beat the whipping cream with the brown sugar in a bowl until stiff peaks form. Dissolve the instant coffee in the rum in a bowl; fold into the whipped cream. Spread evenly over the chilled filling. Garnish with chocolate shavings.

Yield: 8 to 10 servings

Fudge Pie with Raspberry Coulis

PIE

4 ounces unsweetened chocolate

1 cup (2 sticks) butter

2 cups sugar

1 cup chopped pecans

4 eggs

1/4 cup flour

2 teaspoons vanilla extract

RASPBERRY COULIS

12 ounces fresh raspberries

2 tablespoons sugar

Rum or orange liqueur
   to taste (optional)

Whipped topping for garnish

Additional raspberries and fresh
   mint leaves for garnish

For the pie, melt the chocolate and butter in a saucepan. Stir in the sugar, pecans, eggs, flour and vanilla. Pour into 2 greased pie plates. Place in a cold oven. Turn the oven setting to 325 degrees. Bake for 30 minutes. Refrigerate, covered, until chilled.

For the raspberry coulis, purée the raspberries with the sugar in a blender or food processor. Strain through a fine sieve into a bowl. Stir in the rum.

Spoon 1 tablespoon of the raspberry coulis onto each of 12 to 16 dessert plates. Top with a slice of pie. Spoon additional coulis over the pie. Garnish with whipped topping, raspberries and mint leaves.

Note: This pie freezes well. The pie is also wonderful topped with strawberries and whipped cream. Another topping option is peppermint ice cream drizzled with chocolate.

Yield: 12 to 16 servings

Need a rapid chill for your wine or Champagne? Use the canister from your ice cream maker. Keep it in the freezer at all times and whether you're in the mood for ice cream or chilled wine, you'll be ready to go, go, go!

Gooey Fudge Pie

2 ounces semisweet chocolate
2 ounces bittersweet chocolate
$1/2$ cup (1 stick) unsalted butter,
    softened
2 eggs
2 tablespoons flour
1 cup sugar
Dash of salt
2 teaspoons vanilla extract
1 unbaked (9-inch) pie shell

Preheat the oven to 350 degrees. Melt the semisweet chocolate, bittersweet chocolate and butter in a saucepan over low heat, stirring until blended. Remove from the heat; set aside.

Whisk the eggs in a mixing bowl. Stir in the flour, sugar and salt. Add the chocolate mixture and mix well. Stir in the vanilla. Pour into the pie shell.

Bake for 25 minutes or until the center is still slightly liquid. Cool on a wire rack. Serve warm with ice cream and caramel sauce. Or chill and serve with whipped cream and toasted sliced almonds.

Photo on page 220.

Yield: 8 to 10 servings

For a fun luncheon, surprise your guests by bringing out a dessert tray filled with different kinds of ice cream bars! Many have not had an ice cream bar since childhood, and it will bring much laughter and memories of when the ice cream truck would come around to neighborhoods in the summer. What an easy dessert for a hostess and what a fun time for the grownups to sit around licking ice cream bars!

Congressional Cherry Pie

8 ounces cream cheese, softened
1 (14-ounce) can sweetened
    condensed milk
$1/3$ cup lemon juice
1 teaspoon vanilla extract
1 (9-inch) graham cracker pie shell
1 (21-ounce) can cherry pie filling

Beat the cream cheese in a large mixing bowl until light. Beat in the sweetened condensed milk until smooth. Stir in the lemon juice and vanilla. Pour into the pie shell. Chill for 3 hours or until set. Spoon the cherry pie filling over the top. Chill until ready to serve.

Yield: 8 to 10 servings

Creamy Cheesecake Pie

CRUST

1 1/2 cups graham cracker crumbs

1/4 cup sugar

5 tablespoons butter or
    margarine, melted

FILLING

16 ounces cream cheese, softened

2 eggs

1/2 cup sugar

1 teaspoon vanilla extract

TOPPING

1 cup sour cream

1/4 cup sugar

1 teaspoon vanilla extract

For the crust, preheat the oven to 375 degrees. Combine the graham cracker crumbs, sugar and butter in a bowl and mix well. Pat firmly onto the bottom and up the side of a 9-inch pie plate; set aside.

For the filling, beat the cream cheese, eggs, sugar and vanilla in a mixing bowl until smooth. Pour into the crust. Bake for 20 minutes. Remove from the oven; cool for 15 minutes. Increase the oven temperature to 475 degrees.

For the topping, combine the sour cream, sugar and vanilla in a bowl and mix well. Spread gently over the pie. Bake for 10 minutes. Cool on a wire rack. Cover with foil. Chill for 8 to 10 hours before serving.

Yield: 10 to 12 servings

Peach Crumble Pie

1 cup sugar

1/3 cup flour

1/2 teaspoon ground cinnamon

1/8 teaspoon nutmeg

1/2 cup (1 stick) butter,
    cut into pieces

1 unbaked (9-inch) pie shell

8 large peaches, peeled and cut into
    halves or sliced

Preheat the oven to 450 degrees. Combine the sugar, flour, cinnamon and nutmeg in a bowl and mix well. Cut in the butter until crumbly. Place 1/3 of the crumb mixture in the pie shell. Top with the peaches and remaining crumb mixture. Bake for 10 minutes. Reduce the oven temperature to 350 degrees. Bake for 30 minutes longer.

Note: You may substitute thawed frozen peaches for the fresh peaches.

Yield: 8 servings

Lemon Icebox Pie

CRUST

1 1/2 cups graham cracker crumbs

1/3 cup butter, melted

1/4 cup packed light brown sugar

1/4 cup finely chopped pecans

FILLING

1 (14-ounce) can sweetened
   condensed milk

2 egg yolks

2 tablespoons sugar

Juice of 3 or 4 large lemons

MERINGUE TOPPING

3 egg whites

1/8 teaspoon cream of tartar

6 tablespoons sugar

For the crust, preheat the oven to 350 degrees. Combine the graham cracker crumbs, butter, brown sugar and pecans in a bowl and mix well. Press onto the bottom and up the side of a 9-inch pie plate; set aside.

For the filling, combine the sweetened condensed milk, egg yolks and sugar in a bowl and mix well. Stir in the lemon juice. Pour into the crust.

For the topping, beat the egg whites with the cream of tartar in a mixing bowl until soft peaks form. Add the sugar gradually, beating until stiff peaks form. Spread over the top of the pie.

Bake for 15 to 25 minutes or until the meringue is browned. Cool on a wire rack. Refrigerate until chilled.

Note: If raw eggs are a problem in your area, use meringue powder and follow the package instructions.

Yield: 6 to 8 servings

When cooking with lemon juice, a good rule of thumb is that 1 lemon will yield about 3 tablespoons of juice. Squeeze it through a strainer that will catch the seeds. You'll need about 5 lemons to yield a cup of juice. One lemon will also yield about 1 tablespoon of zest.

Margarita Mud Pie

CRUST

1 3/4 cups chocolate wafer crumbs

1/2 cup (1 stick) butter, softened

FILLING

1/4 cup frozen lemonade
    concentrate, thawed

3 tablespoons tequila

4 teaspoons lime juice

1 tablespoon Triple Sec

2 teaspoons grated lime zest

3 drops of green food coloring

5 cups vanilla ice cream,
    slightly thawed

2 cups whipping cream

2 tablespoons confectioners' sugar

1/2 teaspoon vanilla extract

Thin lime slices for garnish

For the crust, preheat the oven to 350 degrees. Combine the wafer crumbs and butter in a bowl and mix well. Press onto the bottom and up the side of a 9-inch pie plate. Bake for 12 minutes. Cool completely.

For the filling, combine the lemonade concentrate, tequila, lime juice, Triple Sec, lime zest and food coloring in a bowl and mix well. Add the ice cream and blend well; do not let the ice cream melt. Spoon into the crust. Cover with plastic wrap. Freeze for 8 to 12 hours.

Beat the whipping cream with the confectioners' sugar and vanilla in a mixing bowl until stiff peaks form. Cut the pie into wedges. Remove to individual dessert plates. Garnish with a dollop of whipped cream and a lime slice.

Note: This is the perfect dessert to top off a spicy Mexican meal. It may also be assembled in individual dessert cups or ramekins.

Yield: 8 to 10 servings

2005 - *Books from Birth of Middle Tennessee, administered by Vanderbilt Children's Hospital, is launched in collaboration with other community agencies.*

Lamar Alexander's Peanut Butter Silk Pie

1 cup creamy peanut butter

8 ounces cream cheese, softened

1 cup sugar

1 tablespoon butter, melted

1 1/2 teaspoons vanilla extract

1 cup whipping cream

1 (9-inch) chocolate crumb pie shell

1 cup (6 ounces) semisweet
    chocolate chips

1/2 cup milk

3 tablespoons brewed coffee

Combine the peanut butter, cream cheese, sugar, butter and vanilla in a bowl and mix well. Beat the whipping cream in a mixing bowl until stiff peaks form. Fold the whipped cream into the peanut butter mixture. Pour into the pie shell; set aside.

Combine the chocolate chips, milk and coffee in a saucepan. Heat over low heat until the chocolate is melted, stirring occasionally. Pour over the top of the pie. Chill, covered, for 8 to 12 hours.

Yield: 6 to 8 servings

Music City Pumpkin Pie

1 3/4 cups sugar

2 teaspoons ground cinnamon

1 teaspoon salt

1 teaspoon ground ginger

1/2 teaspoon ground cloves

1 (29-ounce) can pumpkin

4 eggs, lightly beaten

2 (12-ounce) cans evaporated milk

2 unbaked (9-inch) pie shells

Preheat the oven to 425 degrees. Combine the sugar, cinnamon, salt, ginger and cloves in a bowl and mix well; set aside.

Combine the pumpkin and eggs in a bowl and mix well. Add to the sugar mixture and mix well. Add the evaporated milk gradually, stirring constantly. Divide evenly between the pie shells.

Bake for 15 minutes. Reduce the oven temperature to 350 degrees. Bake for 35 to 40 minutes longer or until the pies test done.

Yield: 12 to 16 servings

2005 - *The Children's Miracle Network Radiothon is held at the hospital with new radio station partner* 107.5 The River.

225

PEPPERMINT CLOUD—As an alternative to the cream filling, beat $1/2$ cup chilled whipping cream, then add 1 tablespoon confectioners' sugar and beat until stiff. Add 2 peppermint sticks or candy canes that have been crushed and mix gently. Refrigerate until ready to use.

2006 - *Children's Miracle Network, totaling 220 hospitals nationally, celebrates its 23rd anniversary.*

Chocolate Éclairs and Cream Puffs

CHOUX PASTRY

1/2 cup (1 stick) unsalted butter

1 cup boiling water

1 cup unbleached flour

1/4 teaspoon salt

4 eggs

CUSTARD FILLING (FOR ÉCLAIRS)

1/3 cup sugar

2 tablespoons cornstarch

1/2 teaspoon salt

1 cup milk

1 cup half-and-half

2 eggs

1 teaspoon vanilla extract

CHOCOLATE ICING (FOR ÉCLAIRS)

3 ounces unsweetened chocolate

1/4 cup water

2 tablespoons butter

1/4 teaspoon salt

2 cups confectioners' sugar, sifted

1/2 teaspoon vanilla extract

**SWEETENED WHIPPED CREAM
(FOR CREAM PUFFS)**

2 cups heavy whipping cream

2 to 3 tablespoons confectioners' sugar

1 teaspoon vanilla extract

Photo on page 226.

For the pastry, preheat the oven to 450 degrees. Add the butter to the boiling water in a saucepan. Cook over medium heat until the butter is melted, stirring constantly. Add the flour and salt all at once. Cook for 1 minute or until the mixture becomes smooth and forms a soft ball, stirring constantly. Remove from the heat. Add the eggs 1 at a time, beating vigorously after each addition. Beat until smooth. For éclairs, use 2 tablespoons pastry, spreading into a 1×3-inch oblong shape. For cream puffs, drop by tablespoonfuls onto a greased baking sheet. Bake for 15 minutes. Reduce the oven temperature to 325 degrees. Bake for 20 to 25 minutes longer. Cool on a wire rack.

For the éclair custard filling, mix the sugar, cornstarch and salt in a saucepan. Whisk in the milk, half-and-half and eggs. Bring to a boil over medium heat, stirring constantly with a wooden spoon. Remove from the heat. Stir in the vanilla. Cool completely. Split each éclair lengthwise with a serrated knife. Fill with the custard.

For the éclair chocolate icing, combine the chocolate, water, butter and salt in a saucepan. Cook over medium heat until the chocolate and butter are melted. Remove from the heat. Whisk in the confectioners' sugar and vanilla until smooth. Spread over the éclairs.

For the sweetened whipped cream, beat the cream in a mixing bowl to the desired consistency. Beat in the confectioners' sugar and vanilla. Split each cream puff in half. Fill with the whipped cream. Dust the tops with additional sifted confectioners' sugar. Éclairs and cream puffs are best consumed the day they are made.

Yield: 16 éclairs, or 24 cream puffs

Abby's Toffee Blondies

If you find yourself with an abundance of lemons, squeeze them and freeze the juice in an airtight container. You may also freeze the zest, or the yellow part of the skin. Then you'll have it ready when you need it for cooking or baking. Both the juice and the zest can be stored in the freezer for up to 3 months.

BLONDIES

*3/4 cup (1 1/2 sticks) butter or
  margarine, softened*
2 1/4 cups packed brown sugar
2 eggs
1 teaspoon vanilla extract
2 2/3 cups flour
1 teaspoon salt
2 cups (12 ounces) chocolate chips

TOPPING

*1/2 cup plus 2 tablespoons
  confectioners' sugar*
1/3 cup packed brown sugar
1/4 cup milk
2 tablespoons butter

1/3 cup English toffee bits

For the blondies, preheat the oven to 350 degrees. Line a 9×13-inch baking pan with foil; grease the foil. Cream the butter and brown sugar in a mixing bowl until light and fluffy. Add the eggs and vanilla and mix well. Add the flour and salt and mix well. Stir in the chocolate chips. Spread in the prepared pan. Bake for 25 to 30 minutes. Remove from the oven and immediately poke holes with a wooden pick in the hot layer.

For the topping, combine the confectioners' sugar, brown sugar, milk and butter in a saucepan. Bring to a boil over medium-high heat. Boil for 5 minutes. Pour over the hot layer.

Sprinkle with the toffee bits. Cool completely. Lift the bars with the foil out of the pan before cutting. Cut into 20 to 24 bars.

Yield: 20 to 24 bars

The Best Lemon Bars

CRUST

1³/4 cups flour

²/3 cup confectioners' sugar

¹/4 cup cornstarch

³/4 teaspoon salt

³/4 cup (1¹/2 sticks) unsalted
    butter, softened and
    cut into 1-inch pieces

FILLING

1¹/3 cups granulated sugar

4 eggs, at room temperature,
    lightly beaten

3 tablespoons flour

²/3 cup fresh lemon juice
    (3 or 4 large lemons)

¹/3 cup milk

2 teaspoons grated lemon zest
    (2 large lemons)

¹/8 teaspoon salt

Confectioners' sugar for sprinkling

Preheat the oven to 350 degrees.For the crust, butter a 9×13-inch baking pan lightly. Line the pan lengthwise with 1 sheet of parchment paper; dot the paper with butter. Place a second parchment sheet crosswise over the first sheet. Pulse the flour, confectioners' sugar, cornstarch and salt in a food processor until mixed. Add the butter. Process for 8 to 10 seconds or until blended, then pulse until crumbly. Press firmly over the bottom and ¹/2 inch up the sides of the prepared pan. Chill for 30 minutes. Bake for 20 to 30 minutes or until golden brown. Reduce the oven temperature to 325 degrees.

For the filling, whisk the granulated sugar, eggs and flour in a medium bowl. Stir in the lemon juice, milk, lemon zest and salt. Pour over the warm crust. Bake for 20 to 30 minutes or until the filling feels firm when lightly touched. Cool for 30 minutes on a wire rack. Sprinkle with confectioners' sugar. Lift the baked layer with the parchment paper from the pan. Peel the paper away and cut into bars.

Yield: 24 servings

Crescent Cookies

Place single-stem flowers, such as azaleas or peonies, in wine glasses, Champagne glasses, or dessert glasses of various heights. Scatter tea lights among them and run them the length of your table. It's especially festive if you place them on glass placemats so they will really sparkle.

2 cups flour
1 cup (2 sticks) butter, softened
1/2 cup granulated sugar
1 cup chopped pecans
1 teaspoon vanilla extract
Confectioners' sugar for coating

Preheat the oven to 350 degrees. Beat the flour, butter and granulated sugar in a mixing bowl until mixed. Add in the pecans and vanilla and mix well. Shape into 1 1/2-inch crescents; place on a nonstick cookie sheet. Bake for 12 minutes. Coat with confectioners' sugar. Cool on a wire rack.

Yield: 2 dozen cookies

French Lace Cookies

1 cup sifted flour
1 cup finely chopped nuts
2/3 cup packed brown sugar
1/2 cup corn syrup
1/2 cup (1 stick) butter or margarine

Preheat the oven to 325 degrees. Mix the flour and nuts in a bowl; set aside. Combine the brown sugar, corn syrup and butter in a double boiler. Place over boiling water and cook over direct heat until the mixture boils. Remove from the heat. Add the flour mixture gradually, stirring constantly. Drop by teaspoonfuls 3 inches apart onto a foil-lined cookie sheet. (Keep the remaining batter warm over hot water between batches.) Bake for 8 to 10 minutes. Cool on the cookie sheet for 1 minute. Remove the foil by gently pulling away from the cookies.

Yield: 2 dozen cookies

2006 - *The second annual "Week of the Child" is held.*

Lace Oatmeal Cookies

1 cup quick-cooking oats
1 cup sugar
3 tablespoons flour
1 teaspoon salt
1/4 teaspoon baking powder
1/2 cup (1 stick) butter, melted
1 egg, beaten
1 teaspoon vanilla extract

Combine the oats, sugar, flour, salt and baking powder in a bowl and mix well. Add the butter, egg and vanilla and mix well. Chill, covered, for 1 to 12 hours.

Preheat the oven to 325 degrees. Drop by rounded 1/4 teaspoonfuls 3 inches apart onto a foil-lined cookie sheet. Bake on second rack from the top for 8 to 10 minutes. Cool completely on the cookie sheet. Remove the foil by gently pulling away from the cookies.

Yield: 8 dozen cookies

Lindzer Tarts

1 cup (2 sticks) butter or
   margarine, softened
1/2 cup granulated sugar
1 egg
1 teaspoon vanilla extract
2 1/2 cups flour
Confectioners' sugar for coating
1 (18-ounce) jar strawberry preserves
   or other preserves of choice

Cream the butter and granulated sugar in a mixing bowl. Beat in the egg and vanilla. Add the flour and mix well. Divide the dough into 3 portions; shape each portion into a ball. Wrap in plastic wrap. Chill for 1 hour.

Preheat the oven to 350 degrees. Roll 1 ball of dough at a time 1/4 inch thick on a well-floured surface. Cut into rounds with a glass. Use a clean thimble to cut a hole in the centers of half the cookies. Place on an ungreased cookie sheet.

Bake for about 12 minutes. Cool on a wire rack. Coat both sides of the cookies with confectioners' sugar. Spread desired amount of preserves on the solid bottom cookies; cover with the cut-out tops, pressing lightly.

Yield: 2 dozen

Acknowledgments

Cookbook Committee

Peggy Franks, Chairman

Susan Basel, Art/Design

Abby McLemore, Recipe Testing

Claudia McLemore, Research/Non-recipe Text

Terrie Purser, Recipe Development/Coordination

Anne Saint, Entertainment

For generously sharing with us in the creation of this book

Ian and Wendy Burr, Fran Hardcastle, Joanne Nairon

Mary Teloh, Special Collections Librarian

Vanderbilt University, Nashville, Tennessee

Historical Collection, Eskind Biomedical Library

For generously sharing special recipes from their restaurants

Basantes West End, Nashville

Basantes Green Hills, Nashville

Mario's Restaurant, Nashville

Saffire, Franklin

Sandy's Downtown Grill, Franklin

Stoveworks Restaurant, Franklin

Swett's Restaurant, Nashville

Viking Culinary Arts Center, Franklin

The Yellow Porch, Nashville

For generously sharing their time and taste buds as recipe testers

The Brentwood Fire Department, Fire Station Number 2

Food Stylists

Teresa Blackburn and Whitney Kemp, Nashville

With thanks and gratitude for sharing your tips and kitchen klips…

Chef Harry Schwartz

Contributors

Beth Affolter
Tiffany Alday
Lamar Alexander
Connie Allen
Laura Allen
Laurie Alsentzer
Pat Anderson
Sherry Andrews
Judy Aschner
Louise Baird
Kent Ballow
Polly Barber
Sabine E. Barnett
Basantes Green Hills
Basantes West End
Alvin Basel
Kelly Basel
Samantha Basel
Susan Basel
Mrs. Edith McBride Bass
Mary Lee Baysinger
Regina Beahm
Leslee Bechtel
Peggy Bender
Kathy Berry
U.S. Congresswoman
    Marsha Blackburn
Teresa Blackburn
Karen Bouldin
Holly Bowman
Rosalie J. Boyd
Jeanne Bragg
Mayor Tommy Bragg
Linda Brassell
Anna S. Bright
Beth Ann Bright
Kelly Marie Bright
Mary Alice Bright
Amanda Brown
Hilrie Brown
Leslie Brown
Ann Buchanan
Piper Burch
Heather Cain
Eve Callahan
Lisa Campbell
Pam Campbell

Mrs. Monroe Carell, Jr.
Mindy Leigh Carroll
Tammy Carroll
Tricia Carswell
Chickadee Cottage Cookbooks
Karla Christian, M.D.
Julia Thompson Christman
Cherrie Clark
Sara Clark
Deborah Clements
Kim Coakley
Susan Cone
Patsy Cooney
Brooks Corzine
Frances Corzine
Frannie Corzine
Gina Cossey
Julie Hallford Cottrell
Sharlet Cover
Heather Crook
Billirene Crosby
Mackenzie Crowe
Valerie Crowe
Laura Currie
Dolly Dennis
June Denny
Polly Diggs
Jane Dungan
Betty Dunn
Harriett Dunn
Nina Dyer
Elizabeth Ponder Dykstra
Vicki Eastham
Cassie Edenton
Kathryn Edwards, M.D.
Dana Edwards
Thomas A. Ekman
Mary Lane Everett
Robin Faber
Leesa Felker
Mario Ferrari
John Fields, M.D.
Rick Finney
Eleanor Finney
Shannon Finucane
Luis Fonesca
Claire C. Franks

Jane C. Franks
John Franks
Marcia Franks
Peggy Franks
Rhonda Franks
Lee Ann Freeman
Karyn Frist
Jennifer Gaw
Susan Graham
Doug Grindstaff
Rose Grindstaff
Jennifer Haag
Brenda Franks Hale
Caroline Hale
Brenda Hall
Carolyn Hannon
Fran Hardcastle
Lisa Harkins
Cay Harris
Patricia Hart
Patti Hart
Barbara N. Haynes
Jane Haynes
Joyce Heil
Lisa Heltzel
Martha Hjorth
Lisa Hoffman
Laura Hollins
Alice I. Hooker
Tish Hooker
Kathleen Horrell
Katie Horrell
Kay Horrell
Leslie H. Hudson
Patti Hutchinson
Beth P. Huth
Martha Ingram
Pamela Jackson
Brian Jacobs
Judy Jacobs
Dr. Harry Jacobson
Jan Jacobson
Dr. & Mrs. Steve Johnson
Audrey Jones
Mary Lois Jones
Susan Joyce
Jean Keith

Contributors

Terri Kelly
Whitney Kemp
Donna Kestner
Barbara Kinser
Elisabeth Koch
Patricia Kriebel
Robin Kumar
Myrtle S. Lambos
Mrs. Donald Lane
Joy Lehmann
Connie Leifheit
Evan Lemons
Marty Parish Ligon
Sandy Ligon
Sandra Lipman
Susan Lipson
Kristen Lucas
Jill Luna
Lucy Malone
Mario's Restaurant
Julianne Marlar
Trecia Martin
Betty Wayland Mason
Jean Mason
Mrs. Jack C. Massey
Amy Mauldin
Elissa McCoy
Elliott McElroy
Sandra McLellan
Abby McLemore
Claudia McLemore
Mary McMillen
Robert E. McNeilly, Jr.
Patrice Miller
Shelley Money
Karen Morgan
Marlene Eskind Moses
Lynn H. Moss
Jennifer Mueller
Marcia Mullins
Lee Murphy
Sara S. Murrey
Steve Mydelski
Carla Myers
Joanne Nairon
Margaret Neblett
Carla Nelson
Jonell Nicholson

Sara Ochenski
Leola Osier
Jan Overton
RaeAnne Pardue
Becky Parkey
Gayley Patterson
Robin Patton
Melissa Paty
Nancy Phillips
Phil Phy
Jan Pitzer
Russell Pitzer
Cindy Pope
Debbie Powell
Betty Prichard
Linda Primm
Ben Purser
Benjamin S. Purser, III
Cortney S. Purser
Mary Agnes Purser
Terrie Purser
Liz Quarles
Ernestine N. Reeder
Glen P. Reeder
Dean G. Reeves
Suzanne Y. Reiss
Sheila Reuther
Lorie Richardson
Pat Richardson
Jan Riven
Lauren Roady
Kathy Rolfe
Denise Rosen
Saffire
Anne Saint
Becky Samuel
Sandy's Downtown Grill
Shelley Scholl
John Schroer
Marianne Schroer
Harry Schwartz
Pama Sevier
Debbie Shaw
Martha Shepherd
Susan Shepherd
Jackie Shields
Debbie Shmerling
Martha Rose Shulman

Debbie Sloan
Barbara Smith
Betty Smith
Lori Sain Smith
Carol Ann Solesby
Norman Spencer
Harletta Spencer
Ronda Spivey
Chris Steger
Deborah Stillwell
Mary Stodola
Stoveworks Restaurant
David Swett
Swett's Restaurant
Peggy Swift
Dot Taylor
Joyce Taylor
Mary Taylor, M.D.
Eleanor Teasley
Patricia Temple, M.D.
Kim Totzke
Margaret "Marty" Thompson
Beth Throckmorton
Sandee Tishler
Lucinda T. Trabue
Viking Culinary Arts Center
Kathleen Wakefield
Mrs. J. Cliff Walker
Kim King Wall
Rene Ward
Anna Watson
Nancy Waynick
Candie Westbrook
Ray Whitlock
Lella Wilbanks
Mrs. Ann Hendricks Wiley
Christine Williams
Gina Williams
Jerry B. Williams
Lynne Williams
Shannon Franks Woods
Trish Woolwine
Faye H. Wyatt
Jo Ann Yancy
The Yellow Porch Restaurant
Margaret B. Zibart

Index

Accompaniments
Cranberry Orange Relish, 107
Herb Butter, 124
Pita Chips, 28
Savory Tortilla Chips, 39 ❑
Spiced Pecans, 46
Spicy Fried Walnuts, 44
Strawberry Butter, 73
Sweetened Whipped
    Cream, 227

Appetizers. *See also* Dips;
    Salsas; Spreads
Asparagus Roll-Ups, 16
Baby BLT's, 134 ❑
Blue Cheese Puffs, 17
Cheese Wafers, 138
Chèvre Champignons, 22
Chicken Salad in
    Cucumber Cups, 30 ❑
Cold Crab Salad, 35
Creamy Deviled Eggs, 31 ❑
Eastern Shore Crab Cakes, 36 ❑
Goat Cheese Crisps, 23 ❑
Marinated Shrimp, 38 ❑
Mexican Cheesecake, 20 ❑
Nutty Napoleons, 19 ❑
Salmon and Hearts of
    Palm Rolls, 34 ❑
Savory Tortilla Chips, 39 ❑
Smoked Salmon and
    Egg Salad, 33
Smoked Trout Mousse on
    Endive, 33 ❑
Spicy Egg Rolls with Creamy
    Cilantro Dipping Sauce, 29
Tomato and Goat Cheese
    Crostini, 24
Tomato and Onion Tart, 27 ❑

Apples
Anna's Baked Fruit, 88 ❑
Apple Apple Pie, 216
Autumn Bisque, 55 ❑
Caramel Apples, 161 ❑
Crunchy Coleslaw, 135 ❑

Asparagus
Asparagus Roll-Ups, 16
Chandler's Party Salad, 42 ❑
Oven-Roasted Parmesan
    Asparagus, 176 ❑

Avocados
Avocado Salsa, 16
Avocado with Warm Tomato
    and Basil Vinaigrette, 48 ❑

Bacon
Baby BLT's, 134 ❑
Beef Bourguignon, 94
Broccoli Floret Salad, 50
Cabbage with Bacon and
    Gorgonzola, 177
Chèvre Champignons, 22
Craisin Chicken Salad, 136
New Potato Casserole, 183
Saffire's Country
    Green Beans, 181 ❑
Spinach Casserole, 184
Warm Blue Cheese and
    Bacon Dip, 17

Bananas
Best Banana Bread, 76
Buttermilk Pancakes, 70 ❑
Chef Ray's Tropical
    Rock Shrimp Salsa, 38
Pineapple Banana
    Bread, 76 ❑
Smoothie, 154

Beans. *See also* Green Beans
Country Soup Supper, 60
Game Day Chili, 139
Grilled Chicken with
    Black Bean Salsa, 119
Minestrone from
    Basantes, 59 ❑
Oven-Baked Beans, 142
Spicy Egg Rolls with
    Creamy Cilantro
    Dipping Sauce, 29

Tortilla Soup, 57
White Bean Soup, 61
White Chicken Chili with
    Southern Corn Bread, 140 ❑

Beef. *See also* Ground Beef
Beef Bourguignon, 94
Beef Fillets with Marsala, 92 ❑
Beef Fondue from
    Chef Harry, 95
Beef Wellington, 98 ❑
Braised Short Ribs, 101
Country Soup Supper, 60
Open-Faced Tenderloin
    Sandwiches, 143
Ossobuco, 104
Pepper Steak, 96
Reuben Dip, 30
Roasted Tenderloin of
    Beef in Black Pepper
    Sauce, 97
Standing Rib Roast, 100

Beverages
Fresh Pink Lemonade, 135
Grapefruit Margaritas, 84
Iced Tea, 142
"Iroquois Steeplechase"
    Mint Julep, 149
Mimosa, 66
Smoothie, 154

Blackberries
Grilled Marinated Lamb Chops
    with Blackberry Jelly
    Sauce, 110 ❑
The Perfect Blackberry
    Cobbler, 196

Blueberries
Blueberry-Topped
    Cheesecake Bars, 215
Buttermilk Pancakes, 70 ❑
Chandler's Party Salad, 42 ❑
Perfect Blueberry
    Muffins, 71

Blue Cheese
Blue Cheese Puffs, 17
Blue Cheese Salad Dressing, 42
Fall Salad with Maple Mustard
  Vinaigrette, 46
Nutty Napoleons, 19 ❑
Saffire's Ribbon Salad, 44 ❑
  Warm Blue Cheese and
  Bacon Dip, 17

Bouquet Garni, 56

Breads. *See also* Brunch
Angel Biscuits, 74
Best Banana Bread, 76
Buttermilk Corn Sticks, 139
Chocolate Chip
  Pumpkin Bread, 81 ❑
Cranberry Orange Bread with
  Streusel Topping, 77 ❑
Old-Fashioned
  Gingerbread, 78 ❑
Old South Hot Water
  Corn Cakes, 69
Peach Muffins from
  The Chickadee Cottage
  Cookbooks, 72
Perfect Blueberry Muffins, 71
Pineapple Banana Bread, 76 ❑
Popovers, 75 ❑
Poppy Seed Bread, 80 ❑
Pumpkin Bread, 81
Six-Week Bran Muffins, 71
Southern Corn Bread, 140 ❑
Strawberry Bread, 82 ❑
Strawberry Muffins, 73
Sunday Scones, 69 ❑
Yeast Rolls, 74

Brunch
Anna's Baked Fruit, 88 ❑
Bird's Nests, 154 ❑
Buttermilk Pancakes, 70 ❑
Chicken Spectacular, 86 ❑
Decadent French Toast, 66
Egg Soufflé, 83

Fiesta Quiche, 84 ❑
Stuffed French Toast with
  Orange Marmalade
  Sauce, 67
Wheezie's Tea Cakes, 89

Cabbage
Cabbage with Bacon and
  Gorgonzola, 177
Coleslaw, 135
Country Soup Supper, 60
Crunchy Coleslaw, 135 ❑

Cakes
Carrot Cake, 207 ❑
Chocolate Cupcakes with
  Frosting, 164
Chocolate Molten Cakes with
  Raspberry Coulis, 203 ❑
Chocolate Sour Cream
  Pound Cake, 208
Coconut Cake with
  White Glossy Icing, 210
Coconut Pound Cake, 209
Cream Cheese Pound Cake, 209
Italian Cream Cake, 204
Karyn's Spice Cake, 165
Nona's Chocolate Cake, 205
Strawberry Cake, 201
Tennessee Jam Cake with
  Penuche Frosting, 211

Carrots
Beef Bourguignon, 94
Braised Short Ribs, 101
Carrot Cake, 207 ❑
Carrot Soufflé, 178
Chicken Potpie, 158 ❑
Coleslaw, 135
Country Soup Supper, 60
Curried Cream of
  Chicken Soup, 56
Gingered Carrots, 115

Cheese. *See* Blue Cheese;
  Goat Cheese

Chicken
Blackened Chicken
  Salad, 137
Chicken Didi, 121
Chicken Enchiladas, 147
Chicken Marbella, 114
Chicken Potpie, 158 ❑
Chicken Salad in
  Cucumber Cups, 30 ❑
Chicken Scaloppini with
  Mushrooms, 116
Chicken Spectacular, 86 ❑
Chicken Supreme, 115
Craisin Chicken Salad, 136
Curried Cream of
  Chicken Soup, 56
French Boneless Chicken, 117
Grilled Chicken Stuffed with
  Basil and Tomato, 118
Grilled Chicken with
  Black Bean Salsa, 119
Minestrone from
  Basantes, 59 ❑
Pecan Chicken with
  Dijon Sauce, 120
Spice-Rubbed Hen
  with Roasted Root
  Vegetables, 112 ❑
Swett's Famous
  Fried Chicken, 147
The Yellow Porch
  Chicken Salad, 138
Tortilla Soup, 57
White Chicken Chili with
  Southern Corn Bread, 140 ❑

Chocolate
Abby's Toffee Blondies, 228
Big Frances' Chocolate
  Chess Pie, 216
Chocolate Chip
  Pumpkin Bread, 81 ❑
Chocolate Cupcakes with
  Frosting, 164
Chocolate-Dipped
  Treats, 173

Index

Chocolate Éclairs and
Cream Puffs, 227 ❑
Chocolate Frosting, 164
Chocolate Icing, 205, 227
Chocolate Molten Cakes with
Raspberry Coulis, 203 ❑
Chocolate Mousse, 193
Chocolate Peanut Butter
Bonbons, 172
Chocolate Sour Cream
Pound Cake, 208
Coffee Toffee Pie, 218
Frozen Peppermint
Cheesecake, 212 ❑
Fudge, 173
Fudge Pie with
Raspberry Coulis, 219
Fudgy Brownies, 166
Gooey Fudge Pie, 221 ❑
Homemade Milky Way
Ice Cream, 197
Hot Chocolate Sauce, 212
Hot Fudge Pudding, 166
"Iroquois Steeplechase" Pie, 149
KK's Chocolate Chip
Cookies, 168
Lamar Alexander's
Peanut Butter Silk Pie, 225
Margarita Mud Pie, 224
Mario's Tiramisu, 199
Mother's Snowflakes, 172
Nanaimo Bars II, 167
Nona's Chocolate Cake, 205
The Yellow Porch
Chocolate Torte, 200

Cookies
Crescent Cookies, 230
French Lace Cookies, 230
Friends Favorite
Sugar Cookies, 169
Honey Spice Snaps, 162
KK's Chocolate Chip
Cookies, 168
Lace Oatmeal Cookies, 231
Lindzer Tarts, 231

Mother's Snowflakes, 172
Super Sugar Cookies, 171 ❑

Cookies, Bar
Abby's Toffee Blondies, 228
Blueberry-Topped
Cheesecake Bars, 215
Fudgy Brownies, 166
Nanaimo Bars II, 167
The Best Lemon Bars, 229

Corn
Ben's Favorite Dip, 39
Grilled Chicken with
Black Bean Salsa, 119
Grits Soufflé, 189
Morris' Corn Pudding, 178 ❑
Mother's Corn Pudding, 180
Parchment Baked Tilapia with
Corn and Lime, 122 ❑
Tortilla Soup, 57

Crab Meat
Cold Crab Salad, 35
Creamy Hot Crab Dip, 35
Eastern Shore Crab Cakes, 36 ❑

Cranberries
Anna's Baked Fruit, 88 ❑
Cranberry Orange Bread with
Streusel Topping, 77 ❑
Cranberry Orange Relish, 107

Desserts. *See also* Cakes;
Cookies; Pies
Bread Pudding with
Whiskey Sauce, 198
Burnt Cream, 194 ❑
Caramel Apples, 161 ❑
Cheesecake, 214
Chocolate-Dipped Treats, 173
Chocolate Éclairs and
Cream Puffs, 227 ❑
Chocolate Mousse, 193
Chocolate Peanut Butter
Bonbons, 172

Frozen Peppermint
Cheesecake, 212 ❑
Fudge, 173
Homemade Lemon
Ice Cream, 162 ❑
Homemade Milky Way
Ice Cream, 197
Hot Fudge Pudding, 166
Mario's Tiramisu, 199
Old-Fashioned
Strawberry Shortcake, 150 ❑
Peach Cobbler, 162
Peppermint Cloud, 226
Raspberry Mousse, 192 ❑
The Perfect Blackberry
Cobbler, 196
The Yellow Porch
Chocolate Torte, 200
Tish's Mocha Cream
Dessert, 197

Dips. *See also* Salsas
Ben's Favorite Dip, 39
Creamy Hot Crab Dip, 35
Reuben Dip, 30
Spinach Dip with
Pita Chips, 28
Warm Blue Cheese and
Bacon Dip, 17

Eggplant
Roasted Eggplant
Spread, 24
Zesty Eggplant, 180

Fish. *See also* Salmon
Mario's Seafood Soup, 63
New Potato-Crusted Red
Snapper, 125
Parchment Baked Tilapia
with Corn and
Lime, 122 ❑
Seared Ahi Tuna with Fried
Green Tomatoes, 126 ❑
Smoked Trout Mousse on
Endive, 33 ❑

Index

Frostings/Glazes/Icings
Chocolate Frosting, 164
Chocolate Icing, 205, 227
Cream Cheese Frosting, 204, 207
Friends Favorite Cookie
    Icing, 169
Penuche Frosting, 211
Warm Lemon Glaze, 78
White Glossy Icing, 210

Fruit. *See also* Apples; Avocados;
    Bananas; Blackberries;
    Blueberries; Cranberries;
    Lemons; Mangoes; Oranges;
    Peaches; Pumpkin;
    Raspberries; Strawberries
Congressional Cherry Pie, 221
Fall Salad with Maple Mustard
    Vinaigrette, 46
Overton's Lime Salad, 51

Goat Cheese
Chèvre Champignons, 22
Goat Cheese Crisps, 23 ❏
Smoked Trout Mousse on
    Endive, 33 ❏
Tomato and Goat Cheese
    Crostini, 24

Grains
Chicken Spectacular, 86 ❏
Golden Grits Casserole, 83
Grit Cakes, 128 ❏
Grits Soufflé, 189
Old South Hot Water
    Corn Cakes, 69
Wild Mushroom Risotto, 182

Green Beans
Chicken Spectacular, 86 ❏
Saffire's Country
    Green Beans, 181 ❏

Ground Beef
Bolognese Sauce, 103
Easy Meat Loaf, 186

Game Day Chili, 139
Lasagna Bolognese, 102
Spaghetti Casserole, 159

Ham
Pineapple Baked Ham, 104
White Bean Soup, 61

**Lamb Chops with Blackberry
    Jelly Sauce, Grilled
    Marinated** ,110 ❏

Lemons
Fresh Pink Lemonade, 135
Homemade Lemon
    Ice Cream, 162 ❏
Lemon Icebox Pie, 223
Lemon Sugar Snap Peas, 92
The Best Lemon Bars, 229
Warm Lemon Glaze, 78

Mangoes
Chef Ray's Tropical
    Rock Shrimp Salsa, 38
Mango Salsa, 126 ❏
Tropical Mango Salsa, 122

**Marinade for Pork Tenderloin
    or Salmon,** 106

Mushrooms
Beef Bourguignon, 94
Beef Wellington, 98 ❏
Chèvre Champignons, 22
Chicken Didi, 121
Chicken Scaloppini with
    Mushrooms, 116
French Boneless Chicken, 117
Spaghetti Casserole, 159
Wild Mushroom Risotto, 182
Zesty Eggplant, 180

Onions
Italian Onion Soup, 61
Tomato and Onion Tart, 27 ❏
Vidalia Onion Spread, 25

Oranges
Cranberry Orange Relish, 107
Orange Pecan Pie, 149

Pasta
Basantes' Fettucine
    Pancetta, 129
Bow Tie alla Mario, 105 ❏
Couscous, 111 ❏
Lasagna Bolognese, 102
Lasagna Roll-Ups
    Florentine, 131 ❏
Minestrone from
    Basantes, 59 ❏
Once-a-Year Macaroni
    and Cheese, 156 ❏
Pasta and Seafood Salad
    with Basil, 51
President Reagan's
    Macaroni and Cheese, 130
Spaghetti Casserole, 159

Pastry
Choux Pastry, 227
Piecrust, 86

Peaches
Peach Cobbler, 162
Peach Crumble Pie, 222
Peach Muffins from
    The Chickadee Cottage
    Cookbooks, 72
White Peach Vinaigrette, 44

Peas
Andouille Sausage and
    Black-Eyed Peas, 111
Blackened
    Chicken Salad, 137
Bow Tie alla Mario, 105 ❏
Chicken Potpie, 158 ❏
Italian Party Salad, 45
Lemon Sugar Snap Peas, 92
Pasta and Seafood Salad
    with Basil, 51
Spinage Subic, 188

Index

Pies
Apple Apple Pie, 216
Big Frances' Chocolate
Chess Pie, 216
Coconut Cream Pie, 217
Coffèe Toffee Pie, 218
Congressional Cherry Pie, 221
Creamy Cheesecake Pie, 222
Fudge Pie with
Raspberry Coulis, 219
Gooey Fudge Pie, 221 ❑
"Iroquois Steeplechase" Pie, 149
Lamar Alexander's
Peanut Butter Silk Pie, 225
Lemon Icebox Pie, 223
Margarita Mud Pie, 224
Music City Pumpkin Pie, 225
Orange Pecan Pie, 149
Peach Crumble Pie, 222

Pizza Mini Me's, 160

Pork. *See also* Bacon; Ham;
Sausage
Beef Fondue from
Chef Harry, 95
Grilled Pork Chops, 109
Marinated Pork Tenderloin
with Cranberry Orange
Relish, 107
Pork Tenderloin with
Rosemary and Garlic, 106 ❑
Pork Tenderloin with
Sun-Dried Tomatoes, 108
Pulled Pork Barbecue, 146
Whiskey-Grilled
Baby Back Ribs, 145 ❑

Potatoes
Gruyère Potatoes, 184 ❑
New Potato Casserole, 183
New Potato-Crusted Red
Snapper, 125

Poultry. *See also* Chicken
Chandler's Party Salad, 42 ❑

Pumpkin
Chocolate Chip
Pumpkin Bread, 81 ❑
Music City Pumpkin Pie, 225
Pumpkin Bread, 81

Raspberries
Chocolate Molten Cakes with
Raspberry Coulis, 203 ❑
Fudge Pie with
Raspberry Coulis, 219
Raspberry Mousse, 192 ❑

Salad Dressings
Blue Cheese Salad Dressing, 42
Honey Mustard Dressing, 47
Maple Mustard Vinaigrette, 46
Sesame Dressing, 47
White Peach Vinaigrette, 44

Salads
Avocado with Warm Tomato
and Basil Vinaigrette, 48 ❑
Baked Spinach Salad, 50
Blackened Chicken Salad, 137
Broccoli Floret Salad, 50
Chandler's Party Salad, 42 ❑
Chicken Salad in
Cucumber Cups, 30 ❑
Cold Crab Salad, 35
Coleslaw, 135
Craisin Chicken Salad, 136
Crunchy Coleslaw, 135 ❑
Fall Salad with Maple Mustard
Vinaigrette, 46
Fresh Cucumber Salad, 176
Italian Party Salad, 45
Overton's Lime Salad, 51
Pasta and Seafood Salad
with Basil, 51
Picnic Cucumber Salad, 136
Saffire's Ribbon Salad, 44 ❑
Seasonal Mixed Greens Salad
with Sesame Dressing, 47 ❑
Smoked Salmon and
Egg Salad, 33

The Yellow Porch
Chicken Salad, 138
Will's Favorite Salad, 48

Salmon
Longhorn Salmon, 148 ❑
Salmon and Hearts of
Palm Rolls, 34 ❑
Smoked Salmon and
Egg Salad, 33
Tommy's Grilled Salmon, 124

Salsas
Avocado Salsa, 16
Chef Ray's Tropical
Rock Shrimp Salsa, 38
Mango Salsa, 126 ❑
Tropical Mango Salsa, 122

Sandwiches
All-I-Want-for-Lunch
Grilled Cheese
Sandwich, 156
Open-Faced Tenderloin
Sandwiches, 143

Sauces, Savory
Barbecue Sauce, 146
Bolognese Sauce, 103
Creamy Cilantro
Dipping Sauce, 29
Horseradish
Cream Sauce, 100
Red Pepper
Rémoulade Sauce, 36
Rosemary Wine Sauce, 101
Sesame Scallion
Dipping Sauce, 95
Wasabi Ginger
Dipping Sauce, 95
Whiskey Sauce, 145 ❑

Sauces, Sweet
Hot Chocolate Sauce, 212
Orange Marmalade Sauce, 67
Whiskey Sauce, 198

Index

Sausage
Andouille Sausage and
   Black-Eyed Peas, 111
Golden Grits Casserole, 83
Spicy Egg Rolls with
   Creamy Cilantro
   Dipping Sauce, 29

Seafood. *See also* Crab Meat;
   Fish; Shrimp
Butternut Lobster
   Bisque, 62
Mario's Seafood Soup, 63

Shrimp
Chef Ray's Tropical
   Rock Shrimp Salsa, 38
Grilled Marinated Shrimp
   with Grit Cakes, 128 ❏
Marinated Shrimp, 38 ❏
Mario's Seafood Soup, 63
Pasta and Seafood Salad
   with Basil, 51
Shrimp Scampi, 129

Snacks
Caramel Apples, 161 ❏
Caramel Corn, 160

Soups. *See also* Stocks
Autumn Bisque, 55 ❏
Basantes' Butternut
   Squash Soup, 53
Butternut Lobster
   Bisque, 62
Country Soup Supper, 60
Curried Cream of
   Chicken Soup, 56
Game Day Chili, 139
Gazpacho, 52
Italian Onion Soup, 61
Mario's Seafood Soup, 63
Minestrone from
   Basantes, 59 ❏
Tortilla Soup, 57
White Bean Soup, 61

White Chicken Chili
   with Southern
   Corn Bread, 140 ❏

Spinach
Baked Spinach Salad, 50
Chèvre Champignons, 22
Lasagna Roll-Ups
   Florentine, 131 ❏
Spinach Casserole, 184
Spinach Dip with Pita Chips, 28
Spinage Subic, 188
Tomatoes Rockefeller, 186 ❏

Spreads
Aron's Pimento Cheese, 154
Cheese Dreams, 134
Cream Cheese and
   Feta Spread, 19
Green and Red Pepper
   Jelly Spread, 25
Roasted Eggplant Spread, 24
Vidalia Onion Spread, 25

Squash
Acorn Squash Casserole, 185 ❏
Autumn Bisque, 55 ❏
Basantes' Butternut
   Squash Soup, 53
Butternut Lobster Bisque, 62
Spaghetti Casserole, 159
Squash Casserole, 185

Stocks
Basic Chicken Stock, 57
Lobster Stock, 62

Strawberries
Buttermilk Pancakes, 70 ❏
Chandler's Party Salad, 42 ❏
Cheesecake, 214
Chocolate-Dipped Treats, 173
Decadent French Toast, 66
Old-Fashioned Strawberry
   Shortcake, 150 ❏
Smoothie, 154

Strawberry Bread, 82 ❏
Strawberry Butter, 73
Strawberry Cake, 201
Strawberry Muffins, 73

Sugared Pansies, 89

Tomatoes
Avocado Salsa, 16
Avocado with Warm Tomato
   and Basil Vinaigrette, 48 ❏
Blackened Chicken Salad, 137
Fiesta Quiche, 84 ❏
Gazpacho, 52
Grilled Chicken Stuffed with
   Basil and Tomato, 118
Italian Onion Soup, 61
Pepper Steak, 96
Seared Ahi Tuna with
   Fried Green Tomatoes, 126 ❏
Tomato and Basil Tart, 188
Tomato and Goat Cheese
   Crostini, 24
Tomato and Onion Tart, 27 ❏
Tomatoes Rockefeller, 186 ❏

Vegetables. *See also* Asparagus;
   Beans; Cabbage; Carrots;
   Corn; Eggplant; Green Beans;
   Mushrooms; Onions; Peas;
   Spinach; Squash; Tomatoes
Broccoli Floret Salad, 50
Roasted Root
   Vegetables, 112 ❏
Spaghetti Casserole, 159
Sweet Potato Supreme, 183

❏ Recipe Photo